THE
VEGUCATION
OF
ROBIN

THE
VEGUCATION
— OF —
ROBIN

How Real Food Saved My Life

Robin Quivers

with Rachel Holtzman

AVERY

a member of Penguin Group (USA) Inc.

New York

Published by the Penguin Group
Penguin Group (USA) Inc., 375 Hudson Street,
New York, New York 10014, USA

USA · Canada · UK · Ireland · Australia
New Zealand · India · South Africa · China
Penguin Books Ltd, Registered Offices: 80 Strand, London WC2R 0RL, England
For more information about the Penguin Group visit penguin.com

Most Avery books are available at special quantity discounts for bulk purchase for sales promotions, premiums,
fund-raising, and educational needs. Special books or book excerpts also can be created to fit specific needs.
For details, write Penguin Group (USA) Inc. Special Markets, 375 Hudson Street, New York, NY 10014.

Library of Congress Cataloging-in-Publication Data

Quivers, Robin.
The veguction of Robin : how real food saved my life / Robin Quivers.
     p.   cm.
Includes index.
ISBN 978-1-58333-473-7
1. Quivers, Robin—Health.   2. Health.   3. Vegan cooking.   I. Title.
     RA776.Q68   2013   2012039852
         613.2'622—dc23

Printed in the United States of America
1   3   5   7   9   10   8   6   4   2

Book design by Meighan Cavanaugh

ALWAYS LEARNING   PEARSON

To Howard Stern, Kathi Diver, and Susan Schneidermesser.

You gave me the support and love I needed to fight for my life.

CONTENTS

Foreword by Russell Simmons   ix

PART ONE
YOUR VEGUCATION

1. My Wobbly Path to Health   3

2. Fat and Sick Is Not Your Destiny   13

3. You Are What You Eat and Can't Excrete   21

4. Meat, Dairy, and Processed Food: You Can't Build
   Something Living from Something Dead   31

5. Plants: Your Weapon Against Disease   43

PART TWO

EATING TO LIVE

6. Kick It Off with a Detox   *51*

7. Making Friends with Food   *67*

8. Be Good to Yourself   *81*

PART THREE

RECIPES AND KITCHEN KNOW-HOW

9. The Joy of Cooking   *97*

10. Getting Started   *105*

11. Recipes   *109*

Acknowledgments   *231*

Appendix A. Kitchen Basics   *235*

Appendix B. Seasonal Fruits and Vegetables   *237*

Appendix C. Cooking Methods   *241*

Appendix D. Herbs and Spices   *243*

Notes   *245*

Index   *251*

FOREWORD

I'm so thankful Robin asked me to write the introduction to *Vegucation*, because helping spread the word about the benefits of a vegan lifestyle is one of my great passions in life.

I made the decision to stop eating meat about fifteen years ago. Along with my yoga and meditation practices, I've found that adopting a vegan diet has not only drastically improved my health, but also has improved my relationship with the world. These practices helped me eliminate the neediness that, in retrospect, was the cause of so much unnecessary suffering in my life. And there was nothing that I thought I "needed" more, back in the day, than a fresh piece of meat on my plate.

Man, I used to eat so much meat growing up. Beef ribs, pork loins, turkey wings, chicken thighs, and oxtails, you name it. I probably would have gobbled up an elephant's ass if someone had deep-fried it and served it to me.

Thankfully, I woke up and became conscious of the harm that my diet was wracking on both myself *and* the world. Just like Robin woke up and hopefully you'll wake up too if you're still eating meat after reading this book.

I use the term "wake up" because I believe that eating meat actually represents an unconscious behavior. We all know in our hearts that eating meat is wrong—bad for what it does to our bodies and terrible for the suffering it creates for the animals that are killed on our behalf. Yet often until we get a wake-up call like *Vegucation*, we can't hear that truth in our hearts because we're so distracted by the noise of those who would have us believe that eating meat is okay.

If you have already "woken up" and become conscious of the suffering associated with the production of meat, let me assure you that there's plenty in this book for you too, namely some fantastic recipes. I love that not only does Robin make such a strong case for becoming a vegan, but she also shows you *how* to make healthy dishes that will help ensure that giving up meat isn't just a phase you go through, but a decision that becomes a permanent part of your lifestyle.

Robin's sense of urgency in helping people transform their lives is ultimately why this book resonates so strongly with me. Robin and I are both tired of watching our family members and people we grew up with suffer needlessly. We see strokes, high blood pressure, asthma, heart attacks, diabetes, and even cancer all being written off as "part of getting old," rather than being called what they truly are: symptoms of poor diets.

That's why no matter what background you come from or what sort of lifestyle you've been leading up until today, please accept that you CAN change. You don't have to wake up feeling tired anymore. You don't have to feel guilty about the suffering you're inflicting on animals anymore. You don't have to feel bad about how your body looks. Or even worry about how much longer you've got to live on this earth.

You have it within yourself to change. I've done it. Robin's done it. And you can do it too.

And in these pages, Robin is going to show you how.

Russell Simmons

PART ONE

YOUR VEGUCATION

1.

My Wobbly Path to Health

Last May I underwent a twelve-hour surgery for a grapefruit-sized mass, which had taken up residence in my pelvis. That meant that for half a day my insides were pulled out, poked at, rearranged, and put back together again—not your typical routine procedure. So after all that, do you want to know what ultimately saved my life? My *health*. Sure, the brilliant team of doctors and nurses who cared for me deserve some credit, but if I hadn't dedicated the past ten years to changing my life completely, there could have been a very different ending to this story. I would have been struggling to recover in a rehabilitation center instead of going for walks near my shore house. I would have felt isolated and maybe even depressed instead of laughing with friends and doing the things that make me happiest. I would have resigned myself to being a patient instead of a person. Or I wouldn't even be alive.

Consider the shape I was in at forty-nine years old. I'd been limping for eight months because of a knee injury, my shoulder pain would wake me up in the middle of the night, I had to wear a neck brace because of compressed vertebrae, and so went the list. I barely had any feeling in my right arm, my fingers always tingled, and my circulation was so bad that I didn't even register on the heat screen at the bank. I had to use my elbow! I wrote it off as getting old. I was on pills that made me bloated, tired, and crazy for sugar, and because my electrolyte balance was completely thrown off, I couldn't even walk without my muscles cramping. I figured, well, this is what pills *do,* right? Then I'd spend all my time working and sleeping because I didn't have the energy to do anything else. So when I was invited to a wedding in Los Angeles, I didn't know if I'd even fit in a seat— or in the bathroom!—much less be able to enjoy myself.

I'd luckily gotten to LA with my pride relatively intact, but the morning of the wedding some friends of mine called and said, "Hey, we're going out for breakfast—you should come with us!" But all I wanted to do was rest. It had taken everything out of me just to get into that bed all the way from New York, and I was content to stay there. Plus, I needed *the entire afternoon* to get dressed. Going out had become an endurance sport— getting from the shower to getting in some underwear was like a full-body workout. And then there were pantihose! Forget it. I'd need a break after getting one leg in. By the time I finished getting dressed, I'd be so hot, tired, and uncomfortable that I wouldn't want to go anywhere anymore.

By the time I got downstairs, everyone was laughing and having a good time, but I was already calculating how long I needed to stay at the reception so I wouldn't feel guilty about leaving early. When it finally got to the point where I figured no one would notice I'd left, I snuck my way to the door. But as I was skulking across the dance floor, my longtime friends Ralph Cirella and Rebecca Romijn grabbed me and said, "No! You've got to dance with us! We want to have fun with you!" They snatched my hands and started twirling me around. It took everything I had not to start crying. I was in pain, but more than that, I was embarrassed. It hurt that people assumed I wanted to look the way I did. Ralph and Rebecca didn't see me and think, *What's wrong with Robin?* They just assumed that fat, bloated Robin was who I was. That I simply chose to be that way.

When I got back to my room, I thought about how it wasn't as though I'd hit a plateau where my feeling awful had leveled off. It was getting worse and worse and worse. I needed a neck brace just to feel somewhat normal, and forget about sleep because I'd wake my own self up just by moving. I could barely walk, my body had zero ability to acclimate to changes in temperature, and I no longer had any balance. I'd stick my head out my door just to look out and I'd *fall* out. I'd lie there on my back thinking, *How did this happen?* If things continued as they were, I was sure I was heading for the final stop. I was begging for a heart attack or diabetes. *This is how you die,* I thought. *I can't believe this is how I'm going to go out.*

But at that time, I had no solution. I'd been to doctors, I'd been to chiropractors, I'd seen *everybody.* No one could help. All they wanted to do was shoot me up with steroids that made me sick, fat, and tired—and I didn't need meds to feel that way. They kept putting Band-Aids on the problem. I knew there wasn't something wrong with only my shoulder or my neck or my knee—something was wrong with all of me. So I stopped going to doctors altogether and continued deteriorating on my own. And just when I sort of got comfortable languishing in this state, the September 11 attacks happened.

When I heard the reports about how people had to get out of the buildings by walking down hundreds of stairs, all I could think was, *There was no way I would have been able to do that.* I would have had to wait until somebody could have helped me, and by then it would have been too late. I thought about how if I had been in those buildings, I wouldn't have survived. I'd always been a self-sufficient, independent person, but now I was shuffling toward dependence. *You're done,* I told myself. *You're old; life is done for you. You're not really enjoying it anyway.* It wasn't just that I couldn't have fun at a wedding—I couldn't even save my own life.

But I wanted to! I just had no idea how to do it. I knew I had to lose weight, but every time I'd eat something healthy, I'd have horrible cravings for something not so healthy. I'd try tricking myself, figuring if I just didn't eat in the first place, then I wouldn't crave something afterward. I'd end up eating ice cream in the middle of the night.

Around this time David Blaine came in to do the show, and during the interview mentioned the Master Cleanser, where you don't eat anything except lemon juice and cayenne pepper elixirs for twenty-one days. He said he used it before his big stunts to clear his body and mind. I didn't know much more about the program at the time, but I stored it away in my brain and looked it up when I got home. I was intrigued by making do without food for a little while, so the next day I went to the store and bought everything I needed—lemons, cayenne, maple syrup—and planned to start a short cleanse the following morning. It was Saturday at 8 a.m. when I had the first juice and I figured I'd be eating by noon. But amazingly, I made it through the whole day. By the next day I was pretty impressed with myself for not caving, and I felt a *smidge* better. I thought I'd give another day a try, was successful, and felt another *smidge* better. These tiny differences started to add up, and by the fourth day I really started to soar. I had more energy, felt lighter, and I wasn't wracked by cravings. I wasn't even hungry anymore! By the twenty-one-day mark, I was feeling a whole lot better, but my body was also telling me it needed real food.

I knew at this point that it was what I was eating that made me feel so bad in the first place, so now that I needed to actually *eat* again, I panicked. I had no idea what to do, and the tiny Master Cleanser pamphlet didn't offer any insight, so I figured I'd eat whatever I wanted for a week, then go right back on my lemon juice diet for another twenty-one days.

During one of my first seven-day-off cycles, I went to London. By the time I got to the hotel I was starving, so I took a look at the room service menu. *You've been so good doing your twenty-one days,* I thought. *You should celebrate by having a meal you'll really enjoy.* I saw they had lamb, and I *loved* lamb, so I ordered it. It came up, and it was beautiful. I think I had maybe four bites of that lamb before I needed to immediately lie down. It sunk like a rock in my stomach. I crawled up the bed and just lay there and thought, *Wow, that's what it feels like to have that stuff in my system. And that's how hard it is for my body to deal with it.*

I'd always assumed that there was something wrong with me, not my food. I had no idea that I'd never again be able to eat like I used to, that there was no going back. I couldn't just trick my body into suddenly accepting the foods that were making me sick.

What I did know, though, was that people were starting to notice a change. I hadn't told anyone about the program because this wasn't the first time I'd tried to lose weight, and I didn't want anyone chalking this up to yet another one of Robin's crazy schemes to be skinny. I was tired of failing publicly! So I kept my mouth shut. But after three months, there was no hiding that something was up. People were stunned by how different I looked. Aside from one producer—who said, "Robin, what's up with all that deer piss you keep in the fridge?"—everyone was amazed by my transformation. "Wow, Robin's glowing!" they'd say. Or "Boy, Robin, you look beautiful." There was chatter that I'd had some kind of weight-loss surgery—my stomach banded or stapled or some nonsense. I'd lost so much weight that that's what people assumed. One comedian came on the show after not seeing me for a few months and exclaimed, "Who shrunk Robin?!"

I was just happy to be feeling good. I loved being able to go into a store and not have to go to the "Women's" section. I used to shop only twice a year and buy everything I thought I'd need in one go because it was so awful. And then I was haunted by all the catalogs you get when you shop in a plus-size store—Just My Size, Woman Within, Swimsuits For All. *I'm not that!* I'd think. *I'm not joining the club; don't send me these things!* And now I could actually go and shop in the regular people's part of the store.

Then one morning I was in the bathroom, reaching for some Q-tips, and I realized, *My God, that didn't hurt.* I started checking every joint, every cell, every digit, and thought, *I'm completely pain-free!* I went from the doctor telling me he wanted to fuse the vertebrae in my neck to having every symptom completely disappear. It was all gone. And the only thing that I'd changed was what I was putting in my mouth.

But as much as I loved my transformation on the Master Cleanser, I knew it was impossible to do it forever. At this point my body was saying, *Hey, we really need to eat something!* It was craving nutrition, but I still had no idea what to give it. So I ate. And I ate. And I ate. And surely enough, little by little, all the aches and pains came back. I was going through a stressful transition at work, thinking about my job and not myself, and the next thing I knew, I'd done it again. I tried going back to the Master Cleanser, but that wasn't working anymore.

I panicked. I was losing the amazing feeling that I'd had, and I started doing crazy things to try to hold on to it. I tried sweating myself thin in a sauna. I thought I'd just flush the toxins out. When I got in there it was really, really hot, but I figured I was being a wimp. I forced myself to sit in there, and by the time I walked out I felt like I couldn't cool down quickly enough. I jumped in the shower, thinking the cold water would help, but I must have passed out because my legs went out from under me and I landed on my knees. So in my desperate attempt to keep one hand on the incredible healthy feeling I'd had, I totally lost my grip. And now I was injured. I sat around and ate while I recovered, all the weight I'd lost came back, and I was well on my way to once again not being able to run or walk or feel my fingers.

Then one day I was reading an article in the *Daily News* about a book called *21 Pounds in 21 Days: The Martha's Vineyard Diet Detox*. I went out and bought it, and before I could make any sense of it, I got an e-mail from Dr. Roni DeLuz, one of the authors of the book: "Is this Robin Quivers from *The Howard Stern Show*? I'd like to discuss helping you with a detox." It couldn't have been better timing. We made a plan to get started after Memorial Day weekend, since my family was coming up to visit for the holiday. I remember taking them to dinner and trying to figure out what to eat. I decided on a hamburger, and we all joked about how it would be my very last. And while I had no way of knowing that it really would be—and it's kind of disappointing because it wasn't even very good— it was.

That Monday Roni and her coauthor James Hester came over to my house and talked me through what we'd be doing. I had completely depleted my system with the Master Cleanser, so their biggest priority was getting me nutritionally balanced. Instead of the lemon juice and maple syrup that I'd been living on, I'd have fresh vegetable juices throughout the day and a simple vegetable-based soup in the evening. They taught me that I could still achieve the amazing feeling I'd had while using the Master Cleanser but this time boost every calorie with nutritional density.

I felt great, but I *still* couldn't figure out how to integrate whole foods back into my diet. Since starting the Master Cleanser, I'd bounced between twenty-one days of clean living and seven days of not. Between cleanses I had been on vacation to places like Paris and Burgundy and Napa—the food and wine capitals of the world—and could feel the postcleanse glow fading with every bite of steak and buttered bread. I needed to find some balance.

After working with Roni and James, I had a slightly better idea of what foods to eat, but I really felt lost. People would ask if I was a vegetarian, and I'd just say, "I'm trying to figure things out." But I had no clue. That's when I ran into John Salley, the former basketball player, at a charity event in Long Beach. I told him about the trouble I was having, and he—a longtime vegan—told me to consider the guys he used to play with. "They're falling apart," he said. "And look at me." He looked really good. "You can't build something living from something dead," he said, and suggested I talk to a woman named Sara Soulati, who ran a clinic in California. According to John, she had figured out the connection between eating things like meat and dairy and health problems such as heart disease, diabetes, and high blood pressure. I said I'd call, but really I was thinking, *I would have heard about this—I used to be a nurse. I can't learn something from a basketball player!*

SARA USED TO WORK in cardiac care and couldn't help but notice that her patients kept coming back. After having open-heart surgery they weren't cured—they were just temporarily fixed. They'd go back out and do whatever it was that made them sick, and they'd wind up in the same place over and over again. She started doing her own research and eventually set up a clinic in Inglewood, a predominantly black community. She wanted to prove that it's not your race or heredity that causes high blood pressure, diabetes, kidney disease, and heart disease, but your *lifestyle.*

She told me about a machine she'd come across that was developed by guys at Harvard in the fifties and offered a noninvasive way to treat coronary artery disease. She said if I were ever out in the Los Angeles area, she could give me a complimentary demonstration and we could talk more about her findings.

I eventually found some time to go out there and meet with Sara, and she strapped me into her machine. It was as though I had enormous blood pressure cuffs around my legs, which squeezed every time my heart beat. She explained that the machine essentially takes over the secondary function of your heart by pushing all the blood from the bottom of your body back into the heart after it empties. It gives the organ a rest while increasing circulation, so your blood vessels start to develop more highways—more arteries, veins, capillaries. Of course I couldn't really concentrate on that when the machine. Made. Me. Breathe. Like. This. And I'm sitting there with my legs being strangled and Sara talking and talking and talking and I realized, *Oh my God, she's trying to fill my head with all the knowledge she has during this hour-long demonstration.* Except she kept dialing the machine back so that time kept extending. And. She. Was. Lecturing. About. Every. Horrible. Thing we do to ourselves, like what happens when we eat meat, dairy, processed sugar;

what happens to our digestion and circulation, and how these foods are all culprits in causing cancer, Alzheimer's, autoimmune diseases, macular degeneration, diabetes; and how the worst thing that ever happened was that the food and the drugs were put under the same administration. "What do you think you need all the drugs for?" she asked. "Because you're eating the food!" And she went on and on and on and all I could think about was *What do I have to say to get myself out of here?!* At last I said, "Okay! I'll. Be. A. Vegetarian!" And she said, "No! A vegan!" And I said, "Okay!" And she stopped the machine. And that's how I became a vegan—by torture.

I had no idea what that really involved, but I knew I'd figure it out if it meant finally living the life I wanted to live. But when I left Sara's office I was starving, because you're not supposed to eat before using the machine. I ended up roaming aimlessly around a food court, thinking, *What am I going to eat? What am I going to eat? What am I going to eat?* I ended up with a chicken caesar salad.

When I returned home, I did another twenty-one-day detox, figuring I'd flush myself out once and for all and start with a totally clean slate for following Sara's guidelines. When I was ready to eat again, I decided not to focus on what I was getting rid of but instead on what I was going to add back in. I vowed to never put animal products back into my diet and made a point of adding vegetables and other plant-based foods like grains and beans.

I couldn't believe the difference I saw. I'd never had such a dramatic shift in my health—not when I was taking medication, not when I was wearing a neck brace, and certainly not when I was eating whatever I wanted between detoxes. I no longer had to rearrange my entire life around being sick. When I first came to New York, I knew that every time the office cold would go around, I'd get the cold. If someone in the office got the flu, I'd get the flu. I even stopped Christmas shopping because I figured there would invariably be someone with a cold, and I was going to get it. I tried getting a flu shot every year, but I'd still get sick and have to miss more work. And my body had lost the ability to adapt to my environment. As soon as the weather got cold and the heaters went on, I'd need a humidifier just to have a voice. Every winter I'd buy the latest model but never get rid of any others because I was so afraid of being in a dry room. At one point I had five or six humidifiers going at the same time. I'd wake up and the ceiling would be dripping with condensation. It got so ridiculous that one morning I went to turn on the TV and it blew up!

But when I started eating clean, it all stopped. I went back to see the Chinese healer who helped me recover from my knee injury. He started every session by taking my pulse, but this time as he did it he kept glancing at my chart. When he finished he looked at me and said, "How did you get younger?"

Since I first did the Master Cleanser, I haven't missed a day on the air. I can walk through the valley of the flu and suffering and it doesn't touch me. I can sleep no matter the temperature or humidity and wake up feeling fine, no sinus problems, nothing. And when I was out Rollerblading one day and broke my wrist, the doctor took one look at my X-ray and was shocked I hadn't had surgery before. Normally patients with the same kind of—completely normal—wear and tear would come in complaining of aches and pains. But because I'd taken inflammatory foods out of my diet, I felt fine—aside from the broken wrist. I did end up needing surgery to fuse the broken bones, but then the most amazing thing happened: I healed! And quickly! The doctor told me I'd be in a lot of pain and that I'd have to jerk my fingers this way and that just to retain mobility, but two days after the surgery, the swelling was reduced completely and my hand just *moved*. I showed up for the physical therapy that the doctor prescribed, and off the bat my therapist took the first page of exercises, crumpled them up, and threw them away. Then the next week she did the same thing. And the week after. I had healed so quickly and so completely that I forgot to go back for the final checkup. All the worst-case scenarios that my doctor told me I should expect—that the joint in my hand would freeze, that I'd be in pain, that traveling would make it worse—none of them happened. There was no reason for them to because my body was being nourished with the best stuff possible. Had I been eating and living as I had in the past, my hand would still be a mess. But my plant-based diet was helping my body heal.

The same thing happened when I was recovering from surgery last summer. I came out of the operating room at midnight and by eight the next morning I was making calls to friends and family. Other patients thought I was throwing parties in my room because there was always so much laughter. When the physical therapist came by the second day to take me for a walk, I passed her in the hall because I was already up and around. Doctors who came to look at my chart would do a double take when they saw me there, saying, "You look pretty good for someone who just got hit by a truck!" And in just one week I was home and taking care of myself. I went out to restaurants, enjoyed walks, and regained a sense of normalcy. All because my body and its health were there for me.

I used to go to the doctor and hear, "We're going to have to go in there and clean up your knee" or "We're going to need to fuse your vertebrae." The way I was going, I could have had fifty operations! I used to go to the gym and have to say, "I have a bad shoulder" or "I can't be in this position" or "You're going to have to work around that." But now I say, "I can do everything!" And that's a pretty damn good way to live.

A few months after I went to see Sara, I was out for dinner with a group of friends. I was happily munching on my salad and steamed vegetables when the waiter put down this huge thing of jumbo shrimp in front of the man to my right. These things were enormous, almost like lobster tails, and this guy was grabbing his shrimp and throwing them on his plate and sawing them with his knife and he was gnawing them and chewing and chewing and he turned to me, mouth still full of crustacean carcass, and said, "Dontcha feel bad that you can't do *this*?" And I thought, *Yeah, I feel bad for the shrimp!* Because I really didn't feel like I was missing out. I didn't feel bad that I was looking better than I had in almost twenty years. I didn't feel bad that I was no longer relying on doctors or pills or hoping and praying to make it past fifty without a chronic disease. In fact I was feeling pretty good.

2.

Fat and Sick Is Not Your Destiny

When I was little, I would watch my grandmother take a needle and jab it into her leg. My mother explained that she was a diabetic and had to take insulin every day. My grandmother died when I was twelve. By the time my mother was fifty, she too was diagnosed as a diabetic and had to start sticking herself with insulin. My father had high blood pressure and heart disease. I figured there was no way I'd avoid that path—I had the trifecta.

Most of us just accept illness as our lot in life. The older we get, the more aches and pains we have and the closer we are to living out the destiny that we think is dictated by our genes or age. We see ourselves as devolving instead of evolving. When was the last time you ran into someone and he didn't complain about knee pain or a bad back or arthritis or lament that "I've lost that" or "Guess I can't do that anymore" or "I hope I can hang on to what I do have for as long as I can because I know it's going"? Or how about my favorite, "I'm just falling apart"? It seems like everyone I know is always being knocked out of the game with *something*. I recently was sitting at a table with a group of men in their fifties and sixties, and they were going around comparing when they had had their bypass surgeries—like it was some kind of milestone or right of passage. And everyone's got cancer. It's like you get your diploma when you graduate from college, and when you hit middle age you get cancer. It doesn't have to be some natural event that just *happens*. But we accept that.

People assume that the older they get, the crummier they're going to feel. They hear it all the time—their grandparents or parents are walking around saying, "Oh, I used to be able to do that, but now I can't. I guess I'm just getting old." So they think it's inevitable that one day their bodies will fail them. They think it's only a matter of time before their joints don't work the way they're supposed to, their eyes don't work the way they're supposed to, their brains don't work the way they're supposed to, their hearts, their bones, their pancreases, even their cells! I don't like telling people how old I am because I don't want to be defined by other people's expectations. A couple of years ago I started taking Pilates lessons. I'd see my trainer once or twice a week, and she'd put me through all the machines and exercises—pretty rigorous workouts. Around that time *People* magazine ran before-and-after photos of my transformation, and when I came into my next session, my trainer said, "Oh my God—I saw your picture!" And I said, "Yeah, I used to weigh a lot more." And she said, "No, it's your age! If I knew your age I would have never worked you as hard. You're older than my mother and I'd *never* have her do the things you do."

We've gotten really good at just accepting that our bodies will fail us. The same thing happens with what we think of as "everyday conditions." They've become so common that we don't even call them diseases anymore. I have to chuckle when I hear, "Oh, I'm just one of those people who has hay fever" or "I'm just one of those people who gets migraines." And I love some of these new maladies; they're so funny! Restless leg syndrome—what's that? Dry eye syndrome—huh? Acid reflux disease? What happened? The caveman didn't have dry eye syndrome. He didn't have restless leg. And if he did have acid reflux, you can bet he'd never eat what gave it to him ever again. But commercials on TV tell us that not only are these things customary but that there's a pill for that too! So we accept it as our lot in life. We accept that we just have to live with it. Or worse, we assume technology or science will fix it. My sister-in-law Mary kept waiting for doctors to solve her problems. She didn't think she could do anything for herself, and so she just suffered, getting sicker and sicker and sicker until she eventually passed away. It doesn't have to be that way.

When I was twenty-eight, I went to the doctor for a regular checkup. I was in terrible shape—I was overweight, I smoked, I had frequent panic attacks. The doctor told me I had a month to get my blood pressure down, but if that didn't work, I'd need to go on meds. I didn't want to take a pill for the rest of my life, so I put myself on a diet and started a walking program.

It wasn't a straight line from there to total health, but I refused to accept a chronic disease or constant aches and pains as my destiny. I've watched everyone in my family go down that path. I'm the only one who said no. About a year ago, I was walking with my nephew in San Francisco. He was twenty-three at the time, and we were just wandering around the city, climbing up and down the hills. I turned to him and said, "You don't ever want to lose the ability to do this. You never want to look at the hill and think, *I can't do this*." I told him that I wished I could put him in the body I'd had before and then put him in the body I had now because if he could feel the difference, he'd understand exactly what I was talking about. He'd see firsthand all the things he might have thought he'd have to suffer with but he doesn't have to.

From the beginning of my career, I've shared intimate nuances of my life so that others might connect with them. This is no exception. I've certainly aired no shortage of failures when it comes to my short-lived diets, health kicks, and weight-loss schemes; but this time it's different. Now that I've finally figured out how to take control of my health and completely change my life from the inside out, I'm not going to shut up about it. Because one of the things you can't help doing when you really feel good is running up and down the street, grabbing people and shaking them and saying, "There's hope for you yet!" If there's one thing I want you to walk away with from this book, it's this: Your race does not determine whether you're a diabetic, just as your genetics don't make heart disease inevitable. Your age doesn't mean bad knees are a requirement, and limitations and restrictions in your life are not a given. And while you might not have been diagnosed with a "disease" just yet, the absence of a disease doesn't necessarily mean wellness. Look at me—I was plodding along, getting weaker and weaker and weaker, but nobody gave me a diagnosis. I was out of my mind with grief about how badly I was doing and how much life I was missing—but if someone asked me how my health was, I'd say, "Eh, not so good, but at least I don't have a disease!" I couldn't have been more wrong. The things we know how to prevent, we should prevent. There's just no excuse for already being behind the eight ball when something unexpected happens. Trust me, there are enough bad things that can happen without your contribution. If I had followed my family tree, I probably wouldn't be here to give you fair warning. It took taking control of my health to make a difference in my life, and now I'm giving you the same opportunity. Your well-being and happiness are your choice, so why accept anything less than liberating, life-changing wellness?

YOUR NEW MEDICINE: FOOD

My biggest "Aha!" moment for how to save my own life came from watching my cats. They live such long lives, and they don't get constipated or colds or flus like people do. You don't see them hobbling around with canes. Their bones don't decay like ours while they're just walking around; I've never seen a cat go, "Ow! I broke my hip!" And I realized it's because they eat for nutrition—they eat to *live*. Their food—assuming it's the good stuff and not the junk with bone meal and corn syrup—consists of basic nutrients, and they have just enough at each meal to sustain them. They don't wake up in the morning and need coffee and a doughnut to get going or wonder how they can supersize their lunch. They eat what they need. My animals taught me to demand more of my environment. I want the best food I can possibly have—I want it to be fueling me, not fooling me.

Do you remember Bill Clinton being wheeled out of his heart surgeries? He'd lie there looking all gray and almost dead, and it was only a matter of time before he got wheeled right back in again. He was getting the best medical treatment that this country has to offer—and it was killing him! The doctors said his lifestyle had nothing to do with it. But then why did he keep going back? He was in the care of some of the top cardiac physicians in the world, and they were telling him he needed the deluxe Roto-Rooter treatment every couple of years, that there was no avoiding it. But once Mr. Clinton started eating a plant-based diet—one that's based mostly on vegetables, fruits, legumes, and whole grains; and free of meat, dairy, and processed foods—he suddenly didn't look so gray. And he never had another episode.

Thomas Edison once said: "The doctor of the future will give no medicine, but will instruct his patient in the care of the human frame, in diet, and in the cause and prevention of disease." Edison is one of the smartest men who ever lived and we *still* aren't listening to him. The problem is that there are two realities: the one that your doctors create, where taking a pill for the rest of your life while you slowly but steadily deteriorate is a suitable treatment plan; and the one in which you use the foods grown from this very earth to cure just about every ailment you could think up. But this book isn't about advocating that you never eat another cheeseburger. The only thing I advocate is that you are as healthy as you want to be. The only thing I recommend is that you get a body that works for you. That's what this journey is all about.

There is no magic pill out there to make you feel good, no magic solution that some doctor is going to dream up in the future. Nobody healed me. Nobody had a cure for me. Nobody said, "If you take this, you'll get all better." My body healed itself. Because when we're not junking it up with things like meat and dairy and sugar and processed food, and instead are giving it the vitamins and nutrients that it needs to work, *that's what our body does:* It heals. Perfect health is the body's default setting. When I was a nurse and someone came in with a fever, we'd give him some aspirin or something similar to bring that temperature down. But that was all, one and done. We knew that if we could give the body some room to work, it would cure itself. But taking a pill for the rest of your life is not a cure—it's taking a pill the rest of your life in order to sustain poor health. Medicine isn't magic. Oftentimes what Western medicine does best is to remove something altogether. That adenoid is never going to bother you again because it's not there! That knee isn't going to give you grief now because it's plastic! Even our treatment for cancer isn't a cure—it's just a race to kill all the bad cells before the drugs kill you. I'll concede that some medications are truly beneficial—antibiotics and pain medication—but that's it. And those, ironically, are the only two drugs that have a time limit on how long you're supposed to take them. Otherwise Western medicine really just offers you a Band-Aid—

your doctor figures that you got yourself into this fix, so now here's something to help you live with it. But how about we get to the root of the problem? How about we give the body the right tools to heal itself, and then get the hell out of the way.

IF YOU WANT YOUR BODY to work the way it's supposed to, you need to give it the nutrients it needs. You want your immune system at its peak, your organs working efficiently, and your cells carting around oxygen, not a big ass. The solution isn't in a pill; it's in what you *eat*. Think of it this way: If you bought a Ferrari, what kind of fuel would you put in it? You'd put in the best fuel you could possibly find, and you wouldn't complain about how expensive it was because it was the best. You'd drive that car around feeling really proud, and you'd open the hood and show everyone how well you were maintaining it. "See, it looks like it's just off the showroom floor! It drives perfectly!" And when it came time to put more fuel in, you wouldn't put the hose in the tank and then let the gas run over and spill down your car and all over the tarmac of the gas station. No! When the tank was full, you'd carefully turn off the gas, take the hose out, then gently close the cap.

However, when it comes to our own bodies, it's a different story. We put in—well, we don't even care! What's that? Oh, it's some new Krispy Kreme Bacon Cheeseburger thing? Okay, let me taste it! But your body is your Ferrari! And you're putting crap in it! And I'm not just talking about fast food. I didn't get to such a low point by going through the drive-thru every day—though that's certainly one way to do it. Aside from an obsessive ice-cream habit, I was eating foods that are sold to us as being "healthy": yogurt and shredded wheat, foods high in protein, low in carbs, etc. But more on that later. The bottom line is this: You expect your body, like your car, to run really well. And when it doesn't, you blame it, not your maintenance of it.

Many of us have gotten too complacent with how our bodies work. We take pride in how much abuse they are able to withstand; we brag about our benders and binges. For years our bodies have compensated for all the bad things we do, but when our abuse finally does catch up, we think it's our *body's* fault. We blame it for letting us down and not the other way around. But unless you're treating your body like the most precious vehicle you'll ever drive, don't expect it to act like one.

· · ·

CONSIDER THIS BOOK your maintenance manual, or better yet, your health retirement fund. By planning for your wellness as soon as possible, *before* you start to feel your body breaking down, you're putting health in the bank. Don't, however, think of this as a diet book. In fact stop thinking about your weight. Just stop it. This is a *lifestyle*. It's not a temporary fix so you can go back to doing whatever it was you were doing before. This is a way of living. It's a commitment to feeling good, though yes, you'll look good too.

You'll see that your life doesn't have to be limited or restricted in any way, and that you no longer have to just get by or *endure*. You will understand what it feels like to finally maintain yourself at a level that feels good instead of wondering where the decline ends. You can achieve the kind of health and well-being that is, up until this point, unprecedented. It's time to move past the mentality of living with illness or limitations just because it's the way things are—you *can* start to reverse some of the damage you've done to yourself. Look at me; I went from being almost disabled to no longer being defined by the number on my birth certificate. I went from barely being able to get dressed to running a marathon at fifty-eight! And when life threw me a grapefruit-size curveball, my body was up for the challenge.

I'll teach you how eating for your health means letting your body finally revive and rebuild itself. You'll find your natural, perfect weight, you'll have greater mobility and flexibility, and you'll be stronger. Your balance will improve, your eyesight will improve, your memory will improve. You'll have more energy; your joints won't ache; and you'll have an easier time withstanding temperature changes, so the winter isn't as bleak and the summer as dismal. Hormonal shifts like pregnancy and menopause will be smoother, and your quality of life will be better, including your mood. After I started cleansing, the first thing that occurred to me was "Huh, I didn't realize I was depressed!" I had been living at such a low level of energy that I was basically in a chronic state of the blues. But when I started to feel better, I lightened up. I wanted to participate more, see friends, spend time with family.

Around that time I invited a friend's daughter and some classmates to my house to celebrate their college graduation. There I was with fifteen twentysomethings, and they were treating me like I was one of them—throwing me in the pool, splashing me with water. I was like, "Why are you doing this to me?! I was being nice to you!" But really I was so happy to be included as an equal, not like some middle-aged person they had to be polite to and otherwise leave alone. I was giving off a vitality that made a bunch of kids feel as if I were one of them.

My goal is to teach you how to fuel your car and get your body back to its top shape. First I'm going to help you understand how food affects the way your body works, looks, and feels. Then I'm going to show you which foods hurt and which foods heal. So by the time you get to the amazingly delicious, tummy-full-of-goodness recipes I've collected for you, you'll be ready to look at the meals you eat in a whole new light. This book is not about being a vegan, vegetarian, ovo-lacto whatever. It's much more simple: It's about *vegetables*. It's about getting back into the kitchen, embracing more of the foods that help us flourish, and filling our plates with these hearty, scrumptious plants that really can change your life. I'm not going to tell you that you can't eat the foods you love, but I will give you all the information that you need to make choices that are right for you. And on the other end of all this, if you're being honest with yourself, I can promise that you'll feel younger, lighter, and more alive.

3.

You Are What You Eat
and Can't Excrete

Think of your body as a spaceship. Remember Apollo 13 after *"Houston, we have a problem,"* when the guys on the ground were scrambling to think of solutions? They were finding ways to use whatever resources were available in that little capsule to shunt oxygen from one area to another area and save those astronauts' asses. That's exactly what a body does. You're a capsule, and all you have for resources are the things you carry around with you. Every day your body is playing a game: What can we use to make enzymes? What can we use to clean our system? What do we have that we can use to make fresh cells for our liver? Because your body is always working for you. And despite all your efforts to derail it, it's constantly scouring everything you toss in in order to keep you alive—not necessarily in the peak of health, but alive.

The body is always seeking a stable, constant internal environment, or what's called homeostasis. No matter what you do, it will always try to stay there, comfortably in the middle. This function helps us deal with changes in our external environment, handle stress, and fend off disease. Just like your house's thermostat can sense changes in temperature and then adjust, your body can also sense changes in body temperature, glucose levels, hydration, heart rate, breathing rate, and the presence of pathogens or things that make you sick. When you eat, your body turns into a little biochemist. It takes whatever you've ingested, breaks it down, then diverts those compounds to where they can be used to help maintain homeostasis. It can make fresh blood, build more arterial highways, create new cells—do all the housekeeping it needs to do to keep things running smoothly.

AND YET, WE'RE NOT HELPING. When you give your body something it has a hard time processing, like animal products and processed foods, there's nowhere for this stuff to go. As I told Larry King, "You are what you eat and don't excrete." That's because if you're giving your body foods that are really difficult for it to break down and use, they just sit there. A steak can take up to three days to digest. Think about what would happen if you left a steak on your counter for seventy-two hours. It would rot! And your body isn't exactly refrigerated either. So now it's sitting in you, *decaying*. Your body doesn't want it to gunk up your organs or your bloodstream, and so it hides it. Just tucks it away where no one will see it. It's like that closet or junk drawer you shove everything into when people are coming over. As long as nobody tries to open the door or drawer, everything will appear to be fine. A similar thing happens in your body. Except instead of a closet, that garbage is being stored in your joints and in extra fat cells. And they're not clean, fluffy fat cells, they're dirty, gunky fat cells, full of all the hormones and chemicals that have been pumped into the food you're eating. And It's. Just. Sitting. There. Your ass is not a junk drawer!

Meanwhile, your systems are getting sluggish because they aren't getting the nutrients they need, and all the energy your body does have is being diverted to deal with the junk—instead of rebuilding and healing. Your body can't keep up with processing all that junk, so it stops doing some of its other jobs. Oh your knee's hurting? Sorry, can't heal it. We're busy. We're doing only the essentials right now; anything else will be delayed. Wonder why you get colds all the time or migraines or injuries that won't heal? Because your body is too busy keeping you alive to sweat the small stuff. And so you start to suffer and your quality of life goes out the window.

What's worse is that when your body does need to call on its resources to mend or heal, look at the materials you're giving it to work with. Do you really want your body repairing your organs with a Cheeto?! Think about it. If you're a spaceship and everything you need is in your little capsule, but you're only stocking up on hamburgers, ice cream, Red Bull, and Twinkies, then that's the material your body is grabbing for when it needs to make new cells. Your body is literally rebuilding itself out of junk.

That said, your body is a truly amazing thing. Every time you extend your foot to meet the curb, your body is doing a mathematic calculation to get you there. Remember all those elements and formulas you could never remember in chemistry class? Your body already knew all that stuff! How do you think a drug that's supposed to deal with your mood works? It's in a pill, but it's your body that then goes, *Oh! That's supposed to go to my brain! So let's send it up there.* Some guy in a laboratory is packing that stuff into little tablets, but your body has to get it where it goes. We're all geniuses and we just don't know it. Look at people like Ozzy Osborne, Keith Richards, and Steven Tyler. If a body can survive those guys, a body can do *anything.* If a body can put up with what they were doing and combat it? It's genius! The same goes for us—we get too little sleep, endure too much stress, eat all the wrong things, drink alcohol, take drugs, any number of things— and the body is still willing to give it a go. So how about we do something nice for it?

THE FIRST THING TO understand about your body and wellness is that nothing happens in isolation. If one part is sick, the whole body is sick. That one part didn't get sick on its own. If your coronary arteries are clogged, guess what? All of your arteries are clogged. So nothing is getting the oxygen it needs; things aren't working like they should. People are always saying, "Oh, I have a bad leg" or "I have a bad liver" or "I have a bad heart." And I say, "No, you have a bad *body*!"

But our specialized medical system supports this disjointed thinking. When I became ill, doctors were looking to treat my symptoms—my neck, my shoulder, my knee. *I* was the one who finally realized that something was wrong with all of me. I knew that until I addressed my body as a whole, all those parts that were hurting would never get better. Once I had that one big goal—and not a lot of little ones—I could find that one solution that would help everything get better. When I realized my ill health was the result of what I was eating, I knew I needed to stop relying on foods that were making me sick. The very foods I was ingesting were depriving my organs of the oxygen they needed to keep themselves operating at peak function, causing inflammation that was making my joints ache and preventing my cells from communicating with one another—and I saw that these foods would one day be the cause of any number of diseases that are absolutely preventable. And I finally understood that I needed to be putting foods back in that would give my body fuel to rebuild and heal.

IF YOU WANT TO MAKE a change to your health, your body, and your life, then that all starts here. It starts with learning how the foods you eat can directly help or harm you. As I said before, this isn't about identifying as a vegan or vegetarian—this isn't about labels. What it is about is understanding that the materials you're giving your body to work with make all the difference between *surviving* discomfort, limitations, and a downward spiral of expensive medical care and *living*.

The Truth About Doctors

When you get sick, what's the first thing you do? Probably go to the doctor, right? He or she might give you a few tests, feel around a bit, then send you home with a new medication to add to your collection. That may be fine and well for an illness, but it's not working for our *health*. We've gotten almost robotic about our wellness, like we're on an assembly line and doctors can just plug in what needs to go where. But the truth is, doctors aren't the most important experts who should be involved in your care—*you* are.

I had gotten to the point where I was giving doctors the responsibility for what happened to my body, and that's one of the reasons why I was such a mess. Many of us have totally given our health over to doctors, and we're not willing participants in the process until the moment he makes a mistake, and then we sue him. Like we had nothing to do with it. And that's absolutely, utterly ridiculous. We're not children anymore, and it's time to take responsibility for how we feel. One of the toughest lessons I had to learn was that I had to manage my own ship—and so do you. You're the captain! And you know where medicine has gotten you, or you wouldn't be reading this book.

The issue with giving up all our control to our doctors is that they're not always right. In fact physician error, medication error, and adverse events from drugs or surgery is the *third* leading cause of death in the US, right behind cancer and heart disease. The worst offender, which accounts for almost half those deaths? Complications with medication. And when surgery isn't killing people outright, it's not necessarily helping them either. Take the all-too-common bypass procedure—within three years of an operation, one-third of patients will suffer from chest pain again. Within ten years, half the patients will have died, had a heart attack, or be back to square one with their symptoms. Actually, people who undergo a bypass operation have no fewer heart attacks than those who don't have surgery in the first place. But if surgery isn't addressing the cause of the illness, then why is no one talking about what will?

In traditional medicine, diet and lifestyle routinely take a backseat to drugs and surgery. When was the last time your doctor told you what to eat? Can you imagine what the health care system would look like if doctors were sending away their patients with prescriptions for spinach? The answer is what lies at the root of the health care quandary: No one would be coming back time and time again. Doctors who spent ten, twenty years of their lives learning the most advanced surgical techniques would be undermined by *vegetables*. Far fewer of us would be handing over hundreds or even thousands of dollars on medications or procedures. Insurance and drug companies could no longer hold us hostage. It would be a disaster—for everyone *but* the patients!

This doesn't mean your doctor is a bad person. It just means he or she probably doesn't know any better. Starting in medical school, doctors are taught that the best approaches to health are chemical and mechanical. And drug companies have their hands deep in the medical education system as well, from having medical faculty on their payrolls to sponsoring research grants for drug studies to leading educational seminars that aren't much more than advertisements to paying tens of thousands of dollars in gifts, meals, speaking fees, and lavish trips to lure medical professionals into promoting their products. These companies spend $19 *billion* annually to make sure that by the time these doctors-to-be become practicing physicians and surgeons, they'll remember the good folks who sent their families to Disneyland.

Unfortunately, it's working. All of those pens and notepads and mugs and bagel breakfasts and steak dinners are putting pills in doctors' hands—even if there are no sound medical studies that bolster their efficacy. In one study, 71 percent of doctors were found to believe marketing propaganda over scientific evidence to the contrary. And those overhyped pills are finding their way onto your nightstand.

But the reason why you can walk out of a doctor's office a hundred pounds overweight with a prescription for knee-replacement surgery instead of a nutrition and exercise program is because that's just not what they're trained to do. Doctors are experts in treating symptoms, but when it comes to actually treating diseases that clearly stem from "lifestyle," they're at a loss. Most medical schools require a minimal amount of education on nutrition. Only 25 percent of all accredited medical schools require such a course, and even in those cases, students receive about twenty measly hours of instruction. And so you continue to receive test after test, prescription after prescription, for problems that just won't go away.

The fact is that doctors don't know everything. I just read an article where a doctor interviewed said that professionals in his industry have only enough adequate science to support 85 percent of the medicine they practice. There's a tremendous amount of pressure for doctors to have all the answers, though, and so what do they do? They prescribe. In a recent study, 42 percent of doctors admitted that their patients received too many pills, tests, and procedures. Not because they felt strongly that it was the best course of treatment, but because they were *afraid*. They feared being sued for not "doing enough."

Howard recently came back from the doctor, who recommended he take a low dose of aspirin every day to avoid a heart attack or stroke. I had just read a study that said you shouldn't be doing that, especially if you're healthy, because it doesn't significantly reduce your risk for heart attack or stroke, but it does double your risk of internal bleeding. So I asked him, "Did the doctor tell you you're healthy?" "Yeah." "Well then, why is he putting you on a low dose of aspirin?!" It's like the doctor was admitting that his saying Howard was healthy meant nothing. He didn't even ask about Howard's lifestyle or how he eats; he was making a recommendation based solely on his age and possible predictors. Because the tests and predictors can only guesstimate whether a person will have a heart attack or stroke, doctors need an insurance policy. But then who is suffering? You are!

When doctors prescribe unnecessary drugs and treatments, they expose patients to whole new risks that they didn't have in the first place. Soon it becomes a vicious cycle because the drugs they're now unnecessarily taking are causing unwanted side effects (which are really effects—there's nothing very "side" about a bleeding ulcer or Reye syndrome), for which a doctor may prescribe yet another medication. They're kind of cute, those little pills, and they look innocuous enough. So you figure, *Sure, I'll take that one and I'll take that one*—but you have no idea what they're all doing in there together. It reminds me of when I was in high school chemistry class. After class my lab partner and I would pour all the chemicals we were working with into the test tube to see if the resulting solution would change colors or maybe explode. One time it ate through the glass. That's what I imagine happens with all those pills swimming around in your system. They're eating you! That's why heavily medicated people are often prescribed Prilosec or other GERD (gastroesophageal reflux disease) drugs—to keep their chemical cocktail from eating through their esophagus and stomach.

And if your doctor *does* happen to know about the power of food, it still doesn't necessarily mean that he or she will share it with you. Because so many patients come in wanting the easiest solution—which usually means just slugging down a pill—doctors will most likely assume that you're in that same boat and not explore other avenues. After I swore off doctors and started detoxing, I ran into my old chiropractor at a party. It had been a while since I'd last seen him and he couldn't believe how different I looked. He asked what I'd been doing, so I told him about the cleanses and how I was using food as medicine. Do you want to know what he said? "I didn't know you'd be into that." I told him, "What, you didn't think I'd be into being well?!"

When you're armed with information, you no longer have to guess or capitulate. You won't need to be in the doctor's office all the time asking, "What's wrong with me?" and then be given something to make you shut up. I'm tired of all those doctors who are beating up their patients with their degrees. Before my most recent procedure, I had major qualms about how my surgeon was handling my care. You better believe that I came down hard on him—I didn't owe him any favors! In fact, I realized that he owed *me* a favor. I was giving him the privilege to take care of my most valued possession. I was *allowing* him to treat me. And after I spoke up, he went from dictator-doctor to someone who asked me questions and listened to the answers. We ought to be much more demanding of our medical professionals—it's our right. In chapter 8, I'll talk more about how to find a health practitioner who acknowledges the power of diet and lifestyle, and with whom you can join forces to make your well-being a partnership.

MY NAME IS ROBIN, AND I'M A FOOD ADDICT

At this point maybe you're bargaining with yourself that tomorrow you'll eat better, or next week, or next month. Or maybe you're thinking that now's just not the time to make the change. You have too much going on: too much work, too much stress, too many obligations. Or perhaps you're thinking, *She's not talking about me; I know how to keep my diet under control. I just need a taste of the junk every now and then.*

Consider this your intervention.

Take it from me—I know addiction. For years I was a smoker. I loved how I could have a cigarette in a bar to complement a well-deserved drink, to reward myself while writing my newscast, and to get five minutes of fresh air during the workday. It was social and it felt good, but when it came time to quit, I was able to put my foot down.

Food, on the other hand, was *seductive*. I could eat when no one was looking—it would just be my bed, my ice cream, and me. With cigarettes, I never felt like a man in a desert searching for water, but when it came to ice cream, I *needed* it. I could go home with just one cigarette left in the pack, but if there was only half a pint of ice cream, forget it. If I walked in and my stash wasn't big enough, no matter what time of the night and no matter how tired I was, I had to go replenish it. I tried all the low-fats and the no-fats but it was like methadone—it wasn't nearly as fun. Unless I did *something* to blunt that craving, I wouldn't be able to resist. The flavor was beside the point, really. It was about the mindless mechanical motion of moving the spoon between that pint and my mouth. It was about fantasizing about that initial high that I got when I first started my ice-cream habit, but really just struggling to get enough of a buzz to feel normal.

Food, like heroin or cocaine or alcohol or cigarettes, is a drug. I'll get into the specifics in the next chapter, but know that every time you eat a candy bar, drink a soda, eat a piece of pizza—or let's be honest, half a pizza—you are solidifying food's hold over you. Soon your choices aren't even your choices. Like any addict's, they're your brain chemistry's. But unlike substance abuse, eating food is totally acceptable. Nobody's going to look down on you for eating poorly the same way they would for drinking too much or shooting up. In fact we're *encouraged* to eat foods that aren't good for us, and often by the people who care about us most.

When I was working at NBC, I was walking through the main offices and caught a whiff of something I hadn't smelled in years. My mouth was watering as I followed that smell to the office of one of the sales guys. On his desk was a plate heaped with soul food—fried chicken, chitlins, collard greens with bacon—and he was sitting there, covered in grease, with a huge smile on his face. He told me that he was feeling homesick for the

South and had sought out the foods that reminded him of his family there. This food was *home*. When your mom wanted to show you she loved you, what did she do? She baked cookies. Or maybe she made you macaroni and cheese. Or maybe, if you were really good, you got to go to McDonald's. When we celebrate with our families, what do we do? We eat! Turkey and stuffing at Thanksgiving, ham and deviled eggs at Easter, burgers and coleslaw on the Fourth of July. (Any vegetable in attendance is usually in a casserole, mayonnaise dressing, or cheese sauce.) The food itself becomes affection or comfort or happiness. Except for one thing: It's killing you.

When I was a smoker, I told myself that it was never about the nicotine; it was about the activity. But how ridiculous is that? Every time I took a drag, I was changing my brain's chemistry so that I not only "needed" another cigarette, I needed more cigarettes to feel the initial buzz. The same thing happens with foods that aren't good for us. You'd never know it based on how society has folded these foods into the mainstream, but we're a culture of junkies. We see people who are ill, rely on medication to stay alive, and are in chronic pain because of what they eat—and we're *still* not willing to change our diets. It's like when heroin addicts watch someone OD only to go through his pockets to see if he has any drugs left. "I'll never give up my meat," people say. So I ask you this: Will you choose food over your own life?

4.

Meat, Dairy, and Processed Food: You Can't Build Something Living from Something Dead

EATING ANIMALS

If your childhood was anything like mine, you had to have your glass of milk with dinner. Or you had to finish that pork chop if you wanted dessert. Even now we equate eating meat with being strong and getting lots of iron, and dairy with keeping our bones healthy. They're cornerstones of the recommended American diet and—so we're told— the key to well-balanced nutrition. The only problem is it's not really true. These foods actually do very little to help your body run right, and can harm far more frequently than they can help.

PEOPLE WHO EAT the most animal-based and processed foods get the most chronic diseases. According to the World Health Organization, 80 percent of cardiovascular disease, more than a third of all cancers, and virtually all of the obesity and type 2 diabetes in this country can be linked to a diet high in animal products, such as meat, dairy, and eggs, and processed foods with all its added sugar and fat (we'll get to that in a bit). And, according to a recent study published in *Archives of Internal Medicine,* the more animal you eat, the greater your risk. These foods are clogging up your arteries, raising your blood pressure, and pumping you full of cholesterol, hormones, and antibiotics you don't need. They're also increasing the acidity in your system, which throws off homeostasis and causes inflammation. Inflammation is basically your body misfiring. It thinks it's under attack and so it sends out orders to surround the affected areas and keep everything out while it tries to flush those areas with water. But if you're eating a diet consisting mostly of acidic foods—like sugar, breads, processed or packaged foods, meat, eggs, and dairy—and not enough alkaline foods—like fruits and vegetables—then chances are you're not inflamed in just one isolated place. Back when I was fat and sick, I had so much water in my system that my cells couldn't even meet to exchange information with one another. They were in there yelling, "Helloooo?! Are you there?!" They were drowning. If your cells can't come together to get things done, the whole body starts to shut down, like a chemical plant that's on overload. Except we keep trying to shove chemicals back in, expecting something to change. Inflammation also makes your organs and bones weak because the body has to borrow minerals like calcium, sodium, potassium, and magnesium to neutralize the acid, and it creates the perfect environment for all the common "lifestyle" diseases.

But that's just the beginning. Obesity and diabetes are also gateways to other complications, like stroke, blindness, kidney disease, and, most significantly, cancer. Auto-immune diseases like multiple sclerosis, rheumatoid arthritis, and hyperthyroidism have all been linked to the body confusing undigested animal proteins with foreign invaders. And if you thought your arteries were the only things hardening with animal fat–laden plaque, then think again. Your brain can be affected by too much buildup too. A 2011 study found that people who are overweight and middle-aged have an 80 percent higher risk of developing Alzheimer's and dementia.

Animal-based foods make your ass a junk drawer. As I said before, it's hard for the body to digest meat. Animal-based foods contain no fiber, the key to healthy digestion, and they don't offer the body any nutrients that it can use to make repairs. So instead, meat sits in your body, rotting and leaking all of its cholesterol and toxins into your system (which we'll talk about in just a minute). You'll eventually store it as fat, which is what your body prefers to do automatically with animal proteins, as opposed to burning them off as body heat or using those calories to assist other functions. You can think of it as marbling—just like that nice, juicy steak you ate.

Meat and dairy also make our otherwise neutral systems more acidic. And while the body is perfectly capable of correcting this by using calcium to restore balance, that calcium is pulled from our bones. The more acidic an environment we sustain, the weaker and weaker our bones become, leading ultimately to fractures and/or osteoporosis. But even before that happens, we'll experience joint pain, fatigue, depression, headaches, and immune deficiencies.

The other problem with that Philly cheesesteak decomposing in your gut is that it's also seeping all kinds of hormones and unnecessary antibiotics into your system. The FDA and USDA allow factory farmers to use hormones to promote growth and milk production in their cattle, chickens, and pigs. And because these hormones can sometimes cause infections—and because factory farms are really just huge expanses of crowded animals wading in their own feces, and coincidentally, where 99 percent of all meat raised and slaughtered in the US comes from—factory farmers often mix low doses of antibiotics into animals' feed and water. The problem is that these animals are *your* feed. All the hormones and antibiotics that they ate are now hormones and antibiotics that you're eating. These hormones have been linked to colon and breast cancer, and getting a sustained low dosage of antibiotics through your food can lead to resistance in certain bacteria. And while we're talking about eating what our animals eat, consider the fact that most conventional cattle are raised on starchy grains like corn and soybeans, which fatten them up. But they're not just eating corn and soybeans; they're also eating all the pesticides and fertilizers that those crops have been sprayed with. And now, so are you. Though that seems almost preferable when you consider that it's okay to feed factory-farmed poultry discarded cattle tissue and to feed cattle "poultry litter," or the waste from poultry barns, which in some cases still contains little bits of Bessie.

. . .

Eating animals isn't exactly nice. Before I started on this journey, I never really thought about where my food came from. I knew that a hamburger had at one point been a steer and that chicken wings didn't grow in freezers, but I never stopped to think about what had to happen to get that food on my plate. When you buy a piece of meat, you're essentially financing the operation that produced it. And a lot of the companies that are producing our meat these days are the factory farms responsible for mistreating animals in the name of larger profits. Not only is this a bad thing for your health, it's a bad thing for the planet, and it's especially bad for the animals.

Because of all the energy required to maintain massive feeding operations, food processing—including dairy plants and seafood farms—is the number-one cause of global warming in our food system. Our food system is also a huge contributor to the pollution of rivers, streams, and groundwater. A farm with 2,500 cows produces as much waste as a city of 411,000; but unlike a city, there's no sewage treatment system. Instead manure is piled into cesspools and then sprayed on the land as fertilizer. But the runoff inevitably seeps into places where the bacteria can be harmful to anyone dependent on the water supply.

All this work is being done to preserve a system that is as unsavory as it is unkind. Animals on factory farms are denied all of their natural behaviors. In addition to cows standing knee-deep in their own waste, chickens are packed into cages or large pens and are force-fed weight-promoting hormones that leave them on the verge of structural collapse, keeling over from oversized breasts. Egg-laying hens live in tiny battery cages about the size of a sheet of paper, where they're unable to nest, perch, walk, or even spread their wings. The Humane Society recently released a video they shot undercover in an industrial egg operation, showing horrifying images of chickens crammed together alongside decomposing corpses. Pigs are confined in small concrete pens without bedding or soil or hay for rooting, and during their pregnancies, most sows are kept in "gestation crates" so narrow that they can't turn around or move more than a step or two forward or backward.

In the case of animal cruelty, buying organic doesn't necessarily make that big a difference. Some organic milk comes from factory farms where the cows have never seen a blade of grass. Instead they're fed certified organic grain while hooked up to milking machines. One brilliant company tried to pass off their beef as organic because they were feeding the cows "organic" high-fructose corn syrup!

While I stopped eating animal products for my health, the unexpected result has been an increased awareness in how farmed animals are treated. Howard once said to me, "Think about how high up on the food chain a cow is—they have personalities!" And he's right; we shouldn't be eating personalities. I'm happy and proud that I'm no longer a part of that process and that I can now look at animals with more compassion. In fact I feel more empathy in general. I feel a deeper connection with other people and the world around me.

PROCESSED FOOD: IT'S NOT REAL!

Before we talk about processed food, including sugar, we should really address what food is. By definition it should be something *nutritious*. As a general rule, anything that's in the middle of the supermarket and comes in a box is not food. And anything that no longer looks like what it used to look like as a plant—with the exception of whole grains and legumes—is not food. It's just foodlike stuff.

What happened to our food is similar to what has happened with medicine. When we first started treating ourselves, those remedies came straight from a plant, a root, a leaf, or some bark. And you took that leaf and you applied it wherever you needed it. Then science came along and said, "Let's find out what's in that leaf that makes it so great." They discovered the active ingredient of that leaf and made drugs from that. Then the scientists said, "Well, hey. Now that we know what the active ingredient is, we can derive the chemical formula and just make that in a lab." And so our medicine went from being the remedy itself to being a combination of chemical elements created to mimic that remedy. The moment we took away the plant or root or leaf or bark, though, the remedy didn't do only what it was good for—it did other things too. Your blood pressure medication might give you migraines or your migraine medication might give you high blood pressure. But the scientists and doctors don't call these actual effects; they're just *side* effects.

Similarly scientists are saying, "Let's find out what's in that vegetable that makes it so healthy," and then they try to mimic those nutritional components and deliver them in faux food. So instead of getting the actual nutrients from the plants themselves, we're getting the lab-created version. Grains are now so refined—or stripped of the parts that offer us nutritional benefits—that they need to be "fortified" with the very vitamins and minerals that were there in the first place. The same thing is happening with milk, fruit juice, cereal, and even baby formula. The original nutrient value is no longer there, so it has to be added back in. And just as it happened with our medication, now we're having unintended side effects. It seems that everyone has some kind of allergy or gluten problem, and products that you might have thought were a part of a healthy diet are actually making you sick.

Processed foods are just carriers for sugar and fat. All processed foods—and by that I mean almost anything with a label—are manipulated in some way. Whether it's chemical flavorings, sweeteners, added fats, salt, binders, or preservatives, processed foods are contrived to be as attractive to consumers as possible. Manufacturers have found that we are suckers and addicts when it comes to sugar and fat. It's not really our fault—we're hardwired that way. Back when we ate for survival, and food wasn't always available, our brains adapted to reward us for eating foods that gave us the energy we needed to live, which gave us the incentive to go out and hunt for the foods that did us the most good. This scarcity instinct was a pretty good deal: With every sweet or fatty indulgence, our brain released opioids or endorphins, which have effects similar to cocaine and heroin. Today we no longer need to forage for meals or go for long stretches between them, yet we are still programmed to want sugar and fat, and as studies have shown, we find them as difficult to resist as the drugs themselves.

Companies in charge of selling us food—both at the supermarket and in restaurants—are well aware of this. It's why they add sugar to our bread; cheese and butter to our vegetables; and bacon to *everything*. Because the dangerous truth is that the more sugar and fat we eat, the more sugar and fat we crave.

Processed foods are adult baby food. Food manufacturers and fast-food restaurant companies know that if we can quickly stuff something down our throats, we'll eat more of it. And that's good for the bottom line. Processed foods are actually created so that they're easier to chew and swallow. Most ingredients have been chopped up and then reassembled with additive "glue" like binders and preservatives that further soften the food and help it just slide down the gullet. Perfect if you're on the go! But the problem with breaking down real food, dehydrating it, stuffing it full of additives, and then binding it all together is that it gets really dry. And because food doesn't start to get digested until it's in liquid form, your body won't be readily able to absorb any nutrients that might be holding on for dear life to this cardboard. Add to this quandary that most people are reaching for liquid in the form of sodas, store-bought juices, and energy drinks, which aren't providing the *actual* liquid (read: water) that the body needs. Every time you give your system a search-and-rescue mission to find enough liquid to get this stuff into a usable fluid, you're taking energy away from the more valuable functions your body could be doing.

SUGAR

All that junk will make you sick. So often I hear, "A calorie is a calorie is a calorie." But calories from sugar are different than calories from other foods. Michael Pollan said it best: "The whiter the bread, the sooner you'll be dead." Simple carbohydrates, like those in white bread, crackers, chips, pastries, candy bars, and soft drinks, come from grains or sugar plants but have been so refined that they carry virtually no nutritional benefits. Instead, eating this junk is akin to mainlining glucose, which, like all other processed sugars, will only make you sick. Refined sugar—along with its alter egos dextrose, maltose, evaporated cane juice, and high-fructose corn syrup—takes both you and your body on a roller-coaster ride that taxes all your systems. It causes your blood sugar to shoot up, prompting your pancreas to quickly produce insulin to help get all that sugar into your cells where it can be used as fuel. But if you're eating a bagel for breakfast, turkey on white bread for lunch, pizza for dinner, and sodas and coffee and macchiwhatevers throughout the day—or foods with hidden sugar, like ketchup, mayonnaise, jarred pasta sauce, processed cheese, flavored yogurt, energy drinks, or even junk food that's dressed up as "all natural" or "organic"—then your blood sugar level is high all the time. Your insulin can no longer do its job, and if pushed too far will stop working all together, resulting in type 2 diabetes. And as though we're not already gluttons for punishment, these drastic ups and downs in your blood sugar can cause mood swings and depression, which in most cases make you crave more sugar.

Meanwhile the more sugar you eat, the more acidic your blood becomes, which weakens your entire body. Achy joints, chronic muscle spasms, sluggish organs, and even schizophrenia are linked to an acidic environment. It's also the perfect place for viruses, cancers, and all types of illnesses to flourish. And because your pancreas can't keep up with all the sugar that's now flooding your system, it leaches vital nutrients from your body to help digest it. You're then robbed of iron, calcium, phosphorus, and B vitamins, which can lead to anemia and osteoporosis.

Eating excess sugar—and by excess I mean *no more than 100 calories of added sugar a day for women and 150 for men,* less than in a can of soda!—is also directly linked to cancer. Cells from nearly a third of common cancers, like breast and colon, have what are called insulin receptors. So these cells have the ability to capture insulin from the bloodstream and feed themselves glucose. Imagine that—we've gotten so hung up on sugar that now our cancers have figured out a way to benefit. If you have any of these rogue cells floating around in your bloodstream, eating a diet high in sugar is basically inviting them to an all-you-can-eat tumor buffet.

Perhaps the most obvious consequence of all—and the root of a host of other issues—is that when you eat processed sugar, you get fat. Most people think if they cut out fat from things like cheeseburgers, fettuccine Alfredo, and french fries, they're well on their way to weight loss. But when the liver gets overloaded with sugar, it converts a portion of these calories to fat, some of which ends up as dimples in your butt, thighs, and arms. Then some of it ends up in the bloodstream, where it makes small, dense cholesterol particles—or LDL—that are very good at clogging arteries and causing heart attacks and other cardiovascular diseases. In fact a recent study done by Dr. Kimber Stanhope at the University of California–Davis showed that subjects who went from a healthy diet to consuming high-fructose corn syrup on a regular basis developed elevated LDL cholesterol and other risks for heart disease in *just two weeks*.

SALT

Another problem with processed foods is that they're hiding an obscene amount of salt. Current wisdom dictates that we consume no more than 2,400 milligrams of sodium a day. Do you know how much that is? *One teaspoon*. That's it! And that's not just what you sprinkle on your chicken casserole at dinner; that number includes all the salt you unwittingly take in when you're eating the packaged cardboard that's been stripped of all flavor other than what's artificially added back in. It's not just the obvious offenders like chips and pretzels either. Deli meats and cheeses, canned vegetables, frozen dinners, and even those healthy-looking packaged vegetable juices are all incredibly high in sodium. When you eat too much sodium, you retain water, which stretches your blood vessel walls and causes your blood pressure to go up. As your blood pressure goes up, so do your chances of having a heart attack or stroke.

Sugar Substitutes: Not So Sweet

It's easy to be fooled into thinking that synthetic sugar substitutes offer a more healthful low- or no-calorie alternative to refined sugar. But these laboratory-derived concoctions are as bad as if not *worse* than the alternative. Diet soda, for example—which is one of the worst offenders in the sugar bait-and-switch—has been linked to a familiar litany of offenses. A recent ten-year epidemiological study found that daily consumption of diet soda caused an increased risk for stroke, heart attack, and death. But if you're still not willing to pass on the packets, here are a few things to consider:

- **Aspartame:** Sold as NutraSweet and Equal, aspartame is the Frankensuger that researchers stumbled on during an experiment to create an anti-ulcer drug. Far from nature's own sweet things, it's swathed in all kinds of allegations for causing things like neurological damage to bladder cancer.[*]
- **Saccharin:** The Food and Drug Administration used to require the following warning on Sweet'N Low packets: "Use of this product may be hazardous to your health. This product contains saccharin, which has been determined to cause cancer in laboratory animals." I would think that would be enough said on the matter, though because it was found that the result (of bladder cancer) was unique to rats, the FDA later rescinded its warning and allowed the label to be removed. I'm still not taking any chances.
- **Sucralose:** Otherwise known as Splenda, sucralose is a noncaloric byproduct of actual sugar. In other terms, it's chlorinated sugar. While it has been approved by the FDA, there's a growing amount of anecdotal evidence that dioxins, an unintentional by-product of industrial processes involving chlorine, can cause things like cancer, reproductive and developmental problems, and immune system suppression.[†]

---

[*]Alicia Silverstone, *The Kind Diet* (New York: Rodale, 2009), 48.
[†]Arnold Schecter et al., "Intake of Dioxins and Related Compounds from Food in the U.S. Population," *Journal of Toxicology and Enviromental Health*, Part A, 63 (2001): 1–18, http://www.ejnet.org/dioxin/dioxininfood.pdf.

BETTER SUGAR SUBSTITUTES

As a rule of thumb, less refined sweeteners that take longer to be absorbed into our bloodstream are a much better alternative. Brown rice syrup, stevia, barley malt, agave syrup, maple syrup, and molasses are all healthier choices.

5.

Plants: Your Weapon Against Disease

So at this point you're probably thinking, *Robin, if I shouldn't be eating meat or dairy or anything that comes in a package at the supermarket, then what the heck do I eat?!* The answer is simple: plants! Earlier I talked about how I still managed to hit wellness rock bottom eating foods that most people don't consider to be unhealthy—low-fat yogurt, high-fiber cereal, low-carb anything, etc. The problem was—aside from all the hidden sugar and salt and total lack of nutrition in packaged food—I wasn't eating any *plants*. The things that come out of the ground—vegetables, fruits, whole grains, and legumes—are the good Earth's little miracles when it comes to eating a diet that supports your health. I know it seems crazy, especially when everyone from our parents to our teachers to our government has been drilling into our minds that we need things like meat and dairy to round out our diet, but we just don't need that stuff. The meat and dairy lobbies have pushed hard to fetishize their wares as being the primary sources of protein, calcium, and iron; but when you eat a plant-based diet, you're automatically getting all the vitamins, minerals, and nutrients that you need.* Look at me, I eat only plants, and I haven't died! I haven't come up with some crazy kind of deficiency. In fact I'm healthier than I ever have been in my life. People ask me all the time if I miss eating steak or having cheese with my wine, and the answer is no, I don't. Because when you're reaping the benefits of a plant-based diet, you learn pretty quickly that it's just not worth feeling crummy ever again.

Plants prevent and *reverse* disease—even those diseases thought to be due to genetic disposition. As demonstrated by the groundbreaking research and medical approach of doctors like T. Colin Campbell, Caldwell B. Esselstyn Jr., and John A. McDougall, not only can a plant-based diet prevent illnesses such as heart disease, diabetes, strokes, various cancers, autoimmune diseases, bone disease, kidney disease, and vision and brain disorders in old age, it can reverse their onset. These three men and their combined ninety-three years of research have proven that changing your diet to one that's plant-based can also help you live longer, feel younger, lose weight, lower your blood cholesterol and blood pressure, decrease your need for pharmaceutical drugs and surgeries, have more energy, keep your bones strong, preserve your eyesight, keep your mind sharp, and have a healthier sex life by warding off impotence.

Plants are nature's bodyguards. When plants come under fire from potentially dangerous toxins or "free radicals," they put up a shield. Made out of a chemical blend called antioxidants, these shields soak up the invaders like a sponge. Humans don't have this ability (nor do animals, so don't go thinking that your steak is doing you any of these favors), but when we eat plants, we get their little superhero powers. Free radicals enter our system through all kinds of things—industrial pollutants, too much sunlight, animal-based foods—and they cause serious damage to tissues all over our body. And when tissues start to degrade, they become rigid, which then leads to things like Alzheimer's and

---

*With a couple of exceptions. See "Do I Need to Take Supplements?" (page 46).

dementia, cataracts, hardening arteries, cancer, emphysema, and arthritis. So though we can't ward off free radicals ourselves, luckily the plants we eat take care of it. And because different antioxidants come in different colors (i.e., the yellow beta-carotene of carrots and squash, the red lycopene of tomatoes, the orange beta-cryptoxanthins of oranges), make sure to get the most protection possible by eating a wide variety of fruits and vegetables.

Plants give us the power of fiber. Fiber is an amazing thing, and it's found exclusively in plant-based foods. We don't digest much of it, but it does wonders for us. Fiber pulls water from the body into the intestines to keep things moving along. And because it's like a gunk magnet, attracting all the chemicals and toxins it encounters on its way out, fiber helps us flush out anything that might be harmful to our system. Not getting enough fiber leaves us vulnerable to constipation-based diseases and disorders, including large bowel cancer, hemorrhoids, and varicose veins. Eating a lot of fiber is associated with lower rates of cancers of the rectum and colon and lower levels of blood cholesterol, and it also means feeling fuller while eating less. And because high-fiber foods like whole grains and leafy greens also happen to be high in iron, you're getting a nutrient double whammy.

Plants make you skinny. When you eat a meat-centric, high-fat, high-protein diet, your body retains more calories than you need. When you eat a plant-based diet, your body needs to *use* the calories, not turn them into body fat. So instead of being stored away in your third chin, most of them are delegated to keeping your body warm and stoking your metabolism. In fact people who eat plant-based diets have far fewer issues with their weight, even if they consume the same or even slightly more calories than their animal-eating friends. The carbohydrates you're getting from fruits, vegetables, and grains—when they're unprocessed and unrefined—are complex. That means they not only have a ton of vitamins, minerals, and accessible energy but they take longer for the body to break down. You're not flooding your system with glucose the way you would with chips, candy, and toaster strudels, and you'll feel fuller longer.

Do I Need to Take Supplements?

If you don't already have a specific nutrient deficiency or are older than fifty, then you most likely don't need to take a vitamin supplement. Because nutrition is such a complex biochemical system involving thousands of components that intricately combine to meet your body's needs, there's no way a single pill can imitate a nutrient-packed diet. Just like I described in the previous chapter, mimicking a plant's active ingredients in a lab is a far inferior source of vitamins and minerals than the actual thing. And if you're eating a varied diet made up of all or mostly plant-based foods, you're getting basically all the good stuff that you need. Calcium, iron, and protein—the three that always seem to be a concern when I tell people I don't eat meat—are abundant in and readily absorbed from foods like leafy greens, legumes, nuts, seeds, and whole grains. The two main exceptions are vitamin B_{12} and vitamin D, which can be difficult to get enough of or absorb sufficiently. A deficiency in B_{12}, which comes from bacteria found in the soil that no longer coats our fruits and vegetables at the market, can lead to anemia and neurological disorders, and not enough D— which you're particularly at risk for if you have darker skin—can lead to cardiovascular disease, osteoporosis, cognitive impairment like Alzheimer's, and cancer. You should have your doctor routinely check your levels of these vitamins in addition to ferritin, which is the storage form of iron and gives a more accurate picture of whether or not you're deficient. For a complete list of blood work I recommend, see "An Ounce of Prevention Is Worth a Pound of Cure: How Blood Tests Can Save Your Life" (page 91).

PART TWO

EATING TO LIVE

6.

Kick It Off with a Detox

S hortly after I became a vegan, I went to a party. The hosts had made pierogies from scratch and were so excited about the special vegan batch they'd made for me—and only me. I didn't have the heart to tell them that I was no longer eating things like that—So heavy! And plum pierogis, *really*?—so I did what I thought was the polite thing to do and ate a few. Well, afterward I was a mess. I went to bed feeling bloated and achy and awful. The next day I was telling a friend about the ordeal and he said, "You know what, Robin? Everybody has that experience after they eat a meal, but they just can't feel it anymore."

He was right. We've completely lost touch with what our bodies are telling us. If you wake up with a hitch or a stitch or are feeling a little sluggish, that's your body talking to you. It's your body giving you a report on the general state of things. But if you just shrug and say, "Oh, I guess that's just a sign of age," and pop two aspirin, you're telling your body to shut up. It's like that antismoking commercial that went, "Do you remember when you smoked your first cigarette? You probably coughed your fool head off!" Well you probably did, and that was your body talking to you. It was saying *that's no good*. But if you kept smoking because you thought it was cool or looked tough or you wanted to fit in or look grown up, then eventually that cough went away. Why? Because your body realized you weren't going to listen. So it stopped telling you what it needed. It was a horrible thing that happened—but you thought it was progress!

Remember when I told you how brilliant your body is? Yet you've decided to run it without listening to its innate intelligence. Your body is busy doing calculus that you could never dream of doing on your own, and yet you're telling it, "Don't worry, I got this." Your body's intelligence is what keeps you well. It's what lets you know that your system needs something. That's its *job*. The body just wants to carry you around, to keep you moving. And no matter how badly you've abused the poor thing, it still has the smarts to know how to make things right. It's time you started listening.

Detoxing is one of the best ways to reestablish your connection with your body. Whether it's diving into the deep end and juicing for twenty-one days, eating raw foods for a week or two, or simply adding more vegetables and whole grains to supplement your regular diet, the plans I've outlined below are like a deluxe detailing. All the good stuff from plant-based foods has an opportunity to get in there and clean house. It's creating a blank slate to help you relearn how to listen, how to know when you're really hungry, and what you're really hungry for. Think about it: We start off with very little choice about food. When you were born, they stuck a nipple or a bottle in your mouth and fed you every four hours. Then when you started eating "real" food, you were eating on Mom's schedule. You might have been hungry at 4 p.m., but if dinner was at 6 p.m., you better have waited because that's how civilized people did it. Or maybe you got a snack, but when it was time to sit down to dinner, you were stuck at the table and had to eat everything that was on your plate. You had to please someone else in order for your food intake to be justified, which is how we learn how to eat food—we eat what someone else wants us to eat when someone else wants us to eat it. So we say to ourselves, *One day I'll be able to eat* anything *I want. I'll be in charge of me.* But by that time, we have no clue what we want or what's good for us because that mechanism has been suppressed since birth. We've forgotten what real hunger is.

Our body is naturally inclined to tell us when it wants to eat, what it wants to eat, and how it wants to eat. After a detox you'll finally understand what it means to be truly hungry, as well as what real food tastes like when your taste buds aren't blunted by an overdose of sugar, fat, and salt. It's also an opportunity for your body to begin to heal. Think about your pets when they get sick: You usually can't find them, right? It's because they're resting in a place where you won't bother them. When an animal isn't feeling well, the first thing he'll do is cut back on what he's eating.

When you give your body a vacation from breaking down fatty, sludgy foods and storing the gunk in your already padded organs and loins, you're helping your body move closer to its much-desired equilibrium. You're giving it space to purge all the toxins—be they food-related, environmental, or even emotional—and to rest the digestive system. And because you're freeing up a tremendous amount of energy and resources in the body and simultaneously flooding it with all kinds of vital vitamins and nutrients, your organs and veins and every last cell can start to mend themselves.

Detoxing is about being able to hear your body, understanding your relationship to food, and reinvigorating your body's natural processes. It's a great self-exploration because you spend a lot of time getting to know you. (If you don't want to get to know yourself, then definitely don't detox.) It's even a rest for your brain. You're cutting out all the things that are making you want to stuff yourself silly in the first place. It's a detox from the noise of everyday life.

Below are three different ways to incorporate a detox into your life. You can learn a lot by just adding veggies to every meal, you can learn a lot by going all vegetable, and you learn the most by juice cleansing. I encourage you to work up to the Master Class Juice Detox, but the key to your success will be doing what's realistic. There's no such thing as a bad detox, so do what you're comfortable with and feel all that good veggie love. Whether you're just dipping your toe in or going all the way, read the rest of this section for tips on how to prepare for your detox and get the most out of it.

I'll be giving you the blueprint for how to successfully cleanse for up to twenty-one days, but it's entirely up to you whether you do it. As I said before, I don't advocate anything except getting in tune with yourself and finding out what works for you. This part of the journey is no exception. You can choose to cleanse for a day, a weekend, a week, the full twenty-one days, or anything in between. You might decide to start with a week and then after seven days make the call whether to go longer. Like most things in life, your state of well-being is your choice. You don't want to set yourself up for failure by getting too overambitious about what might be realistic for you—and you certainly don't want to condemn yourself if you do fail (believe me, you're talking to someone who fails all the time)—but failing while knowing your path and failing because you still haven't found it are two different things. My hope is that you'll do whatever it takes to feel good—and to get a body that *works*.

OPTION 1: BABY STEPS

If you've read part 1 and still feel squeamish about going cold turkey, or no turkey, then start by adding before you subtract. Think about making vegetables the star of your meals. Picture the dividers on those plastic picnic plates—most people think the big one is reserved for your meat. But really it's one of the small ones that should corral whatever protein you're adding to your meal. Flip through the recipes in part 3, pick out a few that sound delicious (it might be hard to pick just a few!), and challenge yourself to add a heaping portion of vegetables to each meal. No one said you couldn't have veggies for breakfast. Experiment, take a chance on an unknown plant, mix and match, throw in some whole grains and legumes for variety, and munch with reckless abandon. When you have a plate brimming with colorful, hearty, crunchy/creamy/meaty/juicy/tangy/spicy vegetables, I guarantee that pork chop will start looking a little like overkill.

OPTION 2: VEG OUT

So maybe you're committed to chucking the foods that don't make you feel great, but the idea of having only liquids for twenty-one days freaks you out. If you really want to see what vegetables can do, try eating nothing but vegetables for your detox. Once the detox is over, you can add in as many whole grains and legumes as your heart desires, but this version of a cleanse is an ode to all things veg. You'll be flooding your body with feel-good nutrients that will kick-start the healing process as you gain newfound appreciation for the power of the leafy. The recipes in the next section are the perfect way to get delicious (and good-for-you) ideas on how to tailor your detox to your taste.

OPTION 3: MASTER CLASS JUICE DETOX

If your system is in need of a reboot, then this is the perfect detox option for you. If you want to feel the most vibrant and nourished that you have in years, then this is definitely the option for you. When I started detoxing, I didn't have an option. In fact I was running out of them. All food made me hurt, and I was barreling down a path of damage to my body that could have been irreversible. But when I started adding juice cleanses into my life, I turned it all around. Now anytime I want to give myself a real gift, I detox. And boy has my body thanked me.

Let me first clarify: A fast is abstaining from all food. But a juice cleanse or detox calls for drinking fresh vegetable juices, and plenty of water and tea and having a soup in the evening. At no point will you be surviving on only air. It always cracks me up when people ask me if doing a juice cleanse is dangerous. What's so dangerous about living in a world that's filled with food and choosing not to eat it?! The moment you decide you don't want to do it anymore, you can just go eat something else. How is that dangerous? However, bariatric surgery—which most doctors would recommend for significant weight loss—is an *imposed fast*. And like all surgery, it's dangerous. Because a portion of your stomach will have been removed or stapled or strangled with a small band, there's no going to the refrigerator when you're starving. There's no reversing your decision without major risk—or at all if you've opted for door 1 or 2—even when you're throwing up or you need your esophagus stretched to get the nutrient-replacement horse pills down. My cleanses never have that problem! Because with juice cleansing, you can eat anytime you want. Nobody's tying you to a chair! Nobody's locking you in a room! There's no such thing as a dangerous voluntary detox.

That said, you should still consult with your doctor before getting started, especially if you are on medication. Certain dosages may need to be adjusted, especially once your body starts working at peak function again. But remember, most doctors know so little about nutrition that ultimately *you* have to decide what to do for your own health. For me the choice was pretty simple: Live on pills for the rest of my life, which would have led to only more pills, or change my life. If at some point in this process you think you need a doctor, go to one. But I guarantee that they'll never tell you anything to support your getting better this way. Most doctors will be quick to say, "I told you this wasn't good for you." I want to remind you of something: If you're three hundred pounds, that same doctor will recommend bariatric surgery. And that's a fast you can't reverse—and it doesn't come with an education. No one's going to tell you that stuffing doughnuts into a blender does not constitute health. So you'll be starving *and* you'll be malnourished. A juice cleanse, on the other hand, is pumping concentrated nutrients through your body and helping it repair all the damage. To me, that's the best medicine that money can buy.

GETTING STARTED: SETTING YOUR INTENTIONS

The worst possible reason to detox—or to do anything really—is to lose weight. You can lose weight any number of ways and still be as unhealthy as ever. Your weight is a side effect of your health. If you get your wellness in check, then your weight will follow. But a cleanse is not for aesthetic changes.

I have a friend who came to me and said he'd like help cleansing. He wanted to lose some weight, and I told him that I didn't care about his weight, I cared about his *health*. I told him to leave me alone about it because he wanted it for all the wrong reasons. I said that he'd never get through it without the right rationale. Finally he reconsidered. And after taking stock of his current health and acknowledging that he wasn't happy relying on blood pressure and cholesterol medications, he finally came back and said, "I'm sick and tired of being sick and tired." That's all I needed to hear. He was ultimately amazed at how wonderful he felt, and his doctor—who had written off the detox as hocus-pocus—had to *decrease* his medication doses.

I'd totally forgotten what it was like to "cross over." It's like when you first move into your new house and you know how great it is, but later you have to hear it from someone else because now it's just your house. But going through the process with him, I remembered what it was like the first time I made that commitment to myself. It felt as though I'd finally awakened, like for way too long I'd been asleep. A cleanse is just that—a commitment. You're going to have to make some changes in your life for the next week, twenty-one days, or however long you choose to detox. Remember what brought you to this point in your life—anxiety about your health, frustrations you might have with limitations, the goal to no longer rely on medications or live with nagging discomfort—and dedicate this journey to yourself.

THE WEEK BEFORE YOU BEGIN

Whether you've chosen option 1, 2, or 3, you'll want to be as prepared as possible.

Pare down your diet. Early in my cleansing career I decided to spend a week at We Care Spa, a detox spa in California, with my friend Jody. She was a newcomer to juicing but had watched as I had changed my life and saw how amazing I looked and felt. As we neared the spa in our rental car, she turned to me in a cold panic and pleaded, "Can we at least have a last meal?!"

I wasn't going to deprive her of one final hamburger before the clean sweep, but know that it's in your best interest—and your body's—to not use your cleanse as an excuse to load up on all the foods that were making you sick in the first place. If you've totally committed to doing this, you should start thinning out what you eat instead of having one last hurrah. The idea is to gently transition your body from breaking down and processing complex foods. For all detoxers—yes, even you Baby Steppers could think about it—start cutting out sugar, caffeine, dairy, refined flour products, and alcohol. You want to phase out all the stuff that clogs us up in the first place. If you've chosen Veg Out or Master Class Juice Detox, also use this week to slowly cut down on heavy proteins, such as beef, pork, and chicken. Fish is okay for the first few days, but phase it out by day three. Start adding more cooked vegetables, salads, and juices so that by the end of the week you've scaled down to primarily raw fruits and vegetables (this doesn't apply to you if you're sticking with cooked vegetables for the week). And by the last few days, start eating fewer grains, even the healthy whole ones.

Slow down your physical activity. When you start changing the way you eat, you may feel you have less energy than usual. It can sometimes just be psychological because we've been told that we need a lot more food to power ourselves than we really do, but your system is undergoing a dramatic shift. In order to let your body rest—and not stress it out further by demanding things of it—this is the time to slow down and be gentle with yourself. Don't try to cram in more exercise now just because you won't be very active during your detox. Just take care of yourself so you're ready to start cleansing on day one.

Build a support system. Enlist the aid of others around you so your detox can be as peaceful as possible. Maybe it's having your partner make dinners for the kids or asking a neighbor to run the carpool or shifting a few extra office responsibilities to a coworker. Whatever it is that will make your life easier during this time, don't be afraid to ask for it. Recognize your own value and worth. This is a great exercise in letting the world support you in something that's good for you. And when you're done, you'll come back to all those people you love and care for in much better shape and in a more loving mind-set, and they'll be happy they did it for you.

Stock up. Three days into your cleanse is not when you want to be navigating the grocery store. Use this week to get everything you're going to need. This includes:

- Water: Get the cleanest, freshest, most wonderful water you can find. You want to rest your system as much as possible and not make it sort out toxins. Go with distilled, spring, or filtered water rather than plain old tap.

- Organic vegetables: Check out the Recipes section to see all the ingredients you'll need throughout your detox. If you're juicing, you'll definitely want to make a big pot of my Free-Form Vegetable Stock/Broth (page 118), which you can use to supplement your juices during the day. In all cases, most vegetables are fair game except for starchier varieties like white-fleshed potatoes, corn, and large squashes.

- Herbal tea: Herbal tea is a nice warm treat and also gives you just enough flavor to satisfy if you do get a little hungry. Test a few to find which are your favorites and keep in mind that not all teas fit the bill. Black tea, green tea, and Lipton—all contain caffeine—are not the same as good herbal tea.

- Juicer: Because fresh, homemade juice is one of the best ways to flush your system with pure nutrients, vitamins, and enzymes, I highly recommend making your own, even if you're not doing a full juice cleanse. You can use a blender or food processor, but you'll need to strain out the solids using a cheesecloth or fine-mesh sieve. So to my mind, a good juicer is a superior investment. Look for a model that's simple to use and easy to clean—you don't want to buy some complicated thing that you can never put back together again. There are great inexpensive models out there. Just make sure to look for a single-auger juice extractor that can also handle wheatgrass and more fibrous vegetables.

  Making fresh juice is a beneficial addition to any cleanse, but bear in mind that because they're so nutritionally dense, I consider a juice to be a meal on its own. So if you're eating solid foods during your detox, don't double up.

And on the eighth day, there was cleansing.

What's the Deal with Fruit?

Fruits are actually the most detoxifying foodstuff on Earth because they're so simple. They're full of nutrients and fiber and therefore easy for the body to break down, so they just zip through the system and take things with them on their way out. But we've done so much damage to ourselves that if we let all those toxins go rushing out at once, we couldn't handle it. It would wreak havoc. So we have to modify by using vegetables, which are a much milder way to clean and restore. You'll see that apples and lemons are used in some of the juice recipes, but it's mostly for flavor and in small enough quantities that they don't actually act like a fruit. Avoid all other fruits during your detox, but feel free to add them in to your regular diet. Fruits have been vilified as being too sugary, but because the sugar is a natural source and the fiber slows its absorption—unlike the processed, refined junk—our bodies can handle it.

Not All Juice Is Created Equal

A friend of mine and I were talking about detoxing, and she said, "I drink juice all the time, so that must be good." And I said, "Oh yeah? Where do you get it from?" "From the store—they have this mixture and that mixture. The label says it's fresh!" Fresh?! It probably came off of a truck and has been sitting in that bottle for weeks. How do you call that fresh? The best-quality juice you can get is vegetable-based and homemade. If you're using mostly leafy green vegetables and drinking the juice right after it's prepared, it will be the most nutritious and cleansing. Going to the store and buying juice is not the same. The stuff in the refrigerated section of the grocery store has been processed, pumped full of artificial coloring, and, worst of all, pasteurized, which means that any raw vitamins, minerals, and enzymes have been obliterated.

THE MASTER CLASS PLAN

Let me first say, Welcome to my world. You're about to experience a life-changing shift in how you feel, how you look, and how you see the world. You're on the precipice of a revolution! But in order to get there, you have to have a game plan.

Think of your cleanse as being eight hours a day. That's how long you're awake and drinking juice before you have a detox soup (page 117) in the evening. During this time you want to aim to have a juice every two hours, with the ultimate goal of having thirty-two to sixty-four ounces of juice a day. You can make juices ahead and freeze them, but in order to get the most nutritional value, try to drink them immediately after making them. The juice will naturally heat up in the extraction process, which kills some of the enzymes, and it continues to break down while it sits in your fridge. Hopefully you've made your schedule more manageable during your cleanse so you'll have plenty of time to make your juices and drink them.

It's a good idea to start your cleanse on a weekend so you can give your body time to adjust and also get the hang of your juicing rhythm. I like to alternate between an hour where I have a juice and an hour where I have a glass or two of water. That way I'm sure to get at least four big glasses of water down a day to help flush out my system. Between juices feel free to have an unlimited amount of herbal tea and Free-Form Vegetable Stock/Broth (page 118), which you can drink cool, at room temperature, or warm. For your evening meal, have a bowl of detox soup.

WHAT TO EXPECT DURING YOUR DETOX

The first thing most people say after their first few days of cleansing is, "I can't believe I wasn't hungry!" The truth is, a detox isn't all deprivation and hysteria. We're not doing this to torture you. Because you're getting really solid nutrition and being good to yourself by not making unnecessary demands on your body that require huge amounts of calories, your whole system will start to relax. But first it has to get rid of all the gunk it's been storing in its junk drawers.

By the second or third day, when your body realizes that it doesn't have to be on high alert to process something really foul, it starts doing all the housekeeping that it hasn't had time to do. It starts releasing all that stuff that's been hanging around, and as it's being released back into the bloodstream to be shipped out, you'll actually start to feel it. It's what's called a detox crisis. You might get a headache, feel achy, shaky, lethargic, nervous, or nauseated, but just allow this to happen. Drink some soothing tea or take a nap. This is really why I recommend starting your cleanse on a weekend so you'll make time to adjust and give your body room to find its natural balance again. But whatever you do, don't give in to your cravings! Most people fail in detoxing because they have these sensations and think that having a bite to eat will help them feel better. It doesn't make you better; it just makes that symptom go away. Wherever your body is in unloading all the junk is where it will get stuck if you start prematurely adding heavier, complex foods, or in the case of Master Class detoxers, solid foods. To eat—or eat junk—during your cleanse is to say, "All right, I give up. I'm too weak to allow my body to clean itself and rest and get better."

After a few days your system will start to chill out. Then there's the euphoria. Day four is when most people have the epiphany that they're feeling really, really good. From there you'll sail through the rest of the detox because it just keeps getting better. You think day four is good? Wait until day seven! I remember when I did my first cleanse, by day seven I was bouncing off the wall. I had a huge burst of energy because my body wasn't using all of it just to digest my food. I had no idea I could feel like that! You'll look at other people on the street and think, *Oh my God, I know* exactly *how bad you're feeling, and I never want to feel that way again!*

You'll start to notice things you haven't before, like your habits with food. You might miss eating, but you're not hungry. You might miss chewing, but you're not hungry. Because you'll be discovering so much about yourself during this process, I highly recommend starting a journal. You'll want to remember how you feel and any resolutions you might make. And just as you'll start to release toxins in the body, emotional toxins get released too. Some of these feelings just come and go, but if strong memories or buried issues come back to you during this time, one of the best things you can do is write them down. Don't try to deal with them while you're cleansing, just acknowledge that this particular sensation came up for you and then address it when this journey is over. You'll be better equipped to handle it—or maybe have a completely different take on it—when your body and mind are clear.

Whatever you do, don't get impatient. Because of our Western mind-set about medicine, we think that things should work *immediately*. When you have a cold and you take some over-the-counter junk that tells your body's warning system to go stuff it, you might then feel better right away—temporarily. But health in real life doesn't work that way. So while you will start to feel healthier within the first few days of your cleanse, don't expect dramatic miracles. You didn't go from well to sick overnight, and you won't go back to well that way either. Twenty-one days of cleansing isn't going to reverse forty *years* of abuse. Remember that this is less a fix-all solution than one step toward building a healthier life. Look at me—I'm still working toward creating that for myself. As I always say, I'm a work in progress!

Start a Movement: Colonics

Because the goal of a detox is to flush out all the toxins that are irritating your body's systems, you haven't really detoxed until you've gotten rid of all of it. If you're not having quality bowel movements—and yes, there is a quality to a bowel movement—then all those vegetables and juices won't do you as much good as they can. Most people are constipated these days. God knows what they're doing when they take the newspaper into the bathroom. How long are you going to be in there?! It shouldn't take that long!

The body wants to eliminate, and it wants to do it every day. It gets to rest and clean itself overnight and then expel what it doesn't need in the morning. But if your system is sludgy with animal products and processed foods that have little to no fiber, then your bowels might be slow to catch up by the time you start your detox.

You hear all kinds of fairy tales about someone finding a Barbie shoe or loose change during a colonic, but I can't say that's ever happened to me. Then again, I've never swallowed my toys or my currency. Some people wax poetic about the process, saying their whole lives flash before them. But you're not looking for the Holy Grail here. You're looking for *feces*. Colonics help flush out the colon and intestinal tract, dislodging any toxins, old fecal matter, and undigested items that can make your system sluggish. The beauty of this is that you can actually improve the tone of your large intestine, meaning that your digestive system will eventually start to work well on its own. If you're looking for the deepest cleansing experience that you can get during your juice cleanse, then think about adding a weekly colonic. If you're not comfortable with the idea, drink a quart of water first thing in the morning, which can help initiate elimination.

Don't, however, be tempted to take over-the-counter cleanse products like psyllium. I once went into a health food store and the girl next to me in line was doubled over in pain. She had done a detox-in-a-box and was now all bound up because she wasn't retaining enough water. I told her she needed a colonic to try to get that stuff out of there. Her body couldn't do it on its own because when you take those products with a poor, sluggish large intestine, it can never get the products out. You couldn't get them out with dynamite! Plus, they're typically harsh on your system and can be addictive. A general rule of thumb: Anything that makes you dependent on it isn't good for you— even if it's in a health food store.

Colonics take longer to activate our own natural processes than guzzling Ex-Lax, but think of them as letting your body work toward operating on its own. If it took you years to get this backed up, then you shouldn't expect things to get better overnight. When you're patient, you're making things better for your body in the long run. And eventually your body won't have to be poked or prodded or artificially stimulated in any way.

To find a reputable colonic practitioner who uses the gravity method—a much gentler process than using machinery to force things in or out—go to detoxtheworld .com and check out the "Colon Therapy Directory."

THE IMPORTANCE OF REST

The world we've set up for ourselves is full of stress and noise and exertion and over-stimulation. Consider your detox from food as also being a detox from the demands of everyday life. We think, *Oh, maybe if I work out and detox, I'll lose even more weight!* We're used to jerking ourselves around and forcing ourselves into contrition. But I say, you're not eating, so let's use this time to reacquaint yourself with yourself. I see a lot of people who think, *Hm, I'm not eating so what else can I do? E-mail? Go shopping? Make phone calls?* How about just sitting and taking it all in. Use this time to just *be*. Really absorb what's happening to you. Learn from it. We normally let ourselves rest only when we're sick, but allowing your body to regularly take a break is what keeps it well. During detox your body needs to be able to devote all its energy to cleaning you out and making necessary repairs, and it can't do that with you running around doing errands. Find some stillness, learn that it's okay to be gentle with yourself, understand that rest isn't the same as being lazy—that it's not being selfish—and start to tune in to what your body has to say. It's probably shouting, "Thank You!"

7.

Making Friends with Food

I used to have a really awful relationship with what I ate. I was afraid of food, really. I'd finish a round of cleansing and would be terrified of having to eat again. I hated the way food made me feel and I still didn't understand *how* it contributed to my not feeling well. But after the first detox I did with Roni, she said, "Okay as, we're going to a restaurant so you can have your first meal and I can teach you how to come off a cleanse." I said, "Do we have to?" But then I sat down and ate a salad. And it tasted so good. I thought ordering salad was like penance—it wasn't supposed to be that good! But this time it was like I'd never actually tasted lettuce before. I mean my whole body was enjoying it—it was good all the way down. It was like great sex. You know how great sex isn't just about your genitals, it's about a whole body experience, a spiritual experience? Well, eating that salad was *everything.*

By adding foods back slowly and carefully, you can finally see how food makes you feel, how much of it you really need, and, best of all, what it actually tastes like. A lot of people come out of a cleanse the way they come out of a diet. They think that now they can finally go and gorge on all the stuff that they restricted themselves from eating. Wrong. This is a chance to figure out how you got into the mess you were in before you started. Coming out of a cleanse is just as big an opportunity for changing your relationship with food as the cleanse itself.

Most likely, the foods you've been eating have deadened your taste buds with all the fat, salt, and sugar that's pumped into them. But now you'll be able to experience the full spectrum of flavors that exist outside of factory-made food. Fresh berries will be sweet as candy. Roasted Brussels sprouts will be toasty and crunchy and rich with caramelization. Grilled mushrooms will be earthy and juicy and meaty. A bowl of baked sweet potatoes will be better than any pint of ice cream because you'll be able to actually feel its vitamin A goodness.

As you add foods, try to pinpoint how each affects the way your body works and feels. Remember when I tried stuffing some lamb shank in my gullet? I was exhausted from having to digest that sucker and could feel it every inch of the way down. Your body's been at rest and you want to gently wake it up. You don't want to just dump a bunch of complex, fat-heavy foods into a system that's been detoxing for twenty-one days, or even two days. The last thing you want to do is shock your body back into submission with things that are hard to digest. So reintroduce foods in the reverse order in which you took them out. For example, if you followed the Master Class plan, start with a day of raw vegetables, salads, and detox soup. Then the next day add cooked vegetables, then whole grains, and so on.

Introduce new foods one at a time so you can observe your body's reaction. It's the best way to find out what might not be for you. Keep in mind that you're no longer eating as a sport—you're eating to *live*. Food tasting good is an added bonus and makes meals much more enjoyable, but what you should value above flavor or convenience is nutrition. If you have an adverse reaction to a food or don't like the way you feel, then that's your body telling you that this particular item isn't a good choice and has its consequences. The flip side of this is being able to look at the world of food and honestly say, "I need that." Your body will let you know. You'll actually be able to hear it when it says, "I want that yellow pepper and that green kale and that orange carrot." And you'll go home and have a perfect meal because you're giving your body exactly what it asked for. That's a wonderful way to live.

Also be mindful of how much you need to eat to feel satisfied. After not eating as much as you might normally, you'll find that you can't eat like did before you started cleansing. That's your body regulating itself. You could go back to eating the volume of food that you were inhaling before the cleanse, but you'd be doing that at the risk of once again losing this newfound connection with yourself. Eat slowly, and, more important, *chew*.

As I was having that little salad orgasm with Roni, I realized that I'd never really chewed anything properly in my life. I'd given most things a few decent chomps—maybe more if there was a big chunk of gristle in my meat—then gulped the rest down. Chances are, you're in the same boat. The majority of the foods that people eat, which have most likely been manufactured in some way, don't really need to be thoroughly chewed. They just kind of slide down after you munch a couple of times and then have to be chased with something to drink because you can't make enough spit to liquefy them. It's basically just goop that you've sloshed some water on. Plant-based foods, on the other hand, call for some actual chewing. As you eat fruits and vegetables, digestion starts in your mouth. Saliva has enzymes that begin to break down the food so its nutrients can be released into your system. And once it does make its way down the intestinal tract, it doesn't just go *kerplunk* in your gut; it gets ferried this way and that, depending on what the body needs where.

When you're eating plants, the more you chew, the better they taste, too. That mind-blowing salad was all about the mastication. As vegetables, fruits, whole grains, and legumes break down in your mouth, they release more flavor. Think about that in relation to meat. Gnawing a T-bone, for the record, is not chewing. And God knows what it ever becomes while you're chewing it, but eventually it has no taste. It's like gum after a while—all the juices have run out and now you have this goo that you have to choke down. Vegetables *never* lose their flavor and they *never* make a goo.

Chewing also alerts your brain that you've gotten food. It takes twenty minutes for your brain to realize that your body is eating, so by spending some extra time getting it down, you're giving your brain more time to register that you've had enough to eat. Once we took chewing out of the equation, we also started overeating. Because by the time your stomach feels full, you've already had too much. But now that you're going to be chewing your vegetables until you just can't chew them anymore, you'll reach a point where you can say, "Well that was nice," or "That was enough of that," and not have to unbutton your pants at the end of a meal.

THIS IS WHY YOU'RE HUNGRY

When I detoxed with the Master Cleanser, my treat to myself was watching some television at night. I'd get in bed, burrow into the pillows, and turn on *Everybody Loves Raymond*. There I was, trying to find a little peace, when I'd be assaulted by commercials yelling at me to eat. "Kentucky Fried Chicken! Two for one! Eat this! Eat that!" I had to start taping my shows because even though I was feeling good, and even though I wasn't hungry, after enough fried drumstick drive-bys, that chicken started looking *beautiful*. But no matter what I did, there were people everywhere telling me to eat more junk.

As soon as you stop eating so much food—especially the kind that comes in plastic and cardboard—one of the first things you'll realize is that there are thousands of food prompts in your environment. We are constantly being told to eat. There are billboards and smells from restaurants and then there's the TV. Not including things like product placement in movies and television, the estimated advertising expenditure for restaurants and for food, beverage, and candy companies was $11.26 billion in 2004. When you compare that to the dinky $9.55 million that the National Cancer Institute was spending to get their fruit-and-vegetable-focused 5 A Day for Better Health Program off the ground, it's no wonder that all we can think about is where our next Snickers is coming from.

I also started to notice that people talk about food all. The. Time. I'd be having a conversation with someone and she'd be like, "Where should I go to lunch today? I could go here or I could go there"—she wasn't asking me, she was having a conversation with herself! And it was 9 a.m.! People start to think about their next meal right after they've eaten a meal. After breakfast they're thinking about lunch, and after lunch they're thinking about dinner. We spend all our time talking about food and looking at food and smelling food and watching other people eat food. But once you step away from all this, you can start to understand where the compulsion to eat comes from. And it's usually not from hunger.

When we crave a given food, it often means that our body is out of balance—our chemistry is off. When you're eating a "clean" diet, one consisting of only whole plant-based foods, you can trust the voice that tells you, "I need that brown rice" or "I need that leafy green." But when you're confusing your system with meat, dairy, or processed products, those messages aren't always right. In chapter 3 I explained how the brain rewards us for eating sugary, fatty foods. And once we do eat those foods, our brain wants more of them, making it pretty much impossible for us to think about anything else. So your afternoon Diet Coke and Doritos are actually rewiring your brain to make eating these kinds of foods routine. And when that happens, eating becomes less a choice than a habit. It's not an easy one to break either. A 2010 study by the Scripps Research Institute reported that rats regularly fed high-calorie, high-fat foods soon developed compulsive overeating habits. They needed more and more just to feel the same initial "high" in their brain's pleasure center. Sound familiar? It's the exact pattern the researchers saw when they gave rats heroin or cocaine.

I've definitely been there. I used to act like a heroin addict when it came to food. I know that there is NOTHING compared to a craving. I've often felt like a failure because I didn't want to eat the ice cream but knew I couldn't sleep unless I did. But over time, as you eat fewer and fewer of these foods, your craving for them will fade. I no longer need a freezer stuffed with tubs of Häagen-Dazs—in fact I don't crave the stuff at all.

The important thing is that you recognize what's causing your desire to eat foods that aren't so good for you. When you see the billboard for a McRib or you smell baking bread at Subway or it's "lunchtime" or even if you're just in a bad mood and your routine is to go for those Girl Scout cookies to feel better, all these cues can stimulate that part of the brain that says, "Feed me" or "Soothe me." It's not an easy voice to ignore, but when you can identify *real* hunger, you'll be able to tap into the one voice that's real—the one that wants you to be healthier and happier. After your detox, you will have reinforced your connection with that voice. You'll be able to hear your body's cues again and give yourself what you're truly hungry for.

SO NOW WHAT DO I EAT?

After I met with Sara and vowed to become a vegan, I was adrift. I knew I was going to be eating mostly vegetables, so then I'd think, *Okay, what vegetables are there?* I didn't know about anything but salad. I'd try having some nuts and maybe microwaving a veggie burger, but all I could think was, *There's got to be more than this.* Over the years I'd tried being a vegetarian, but I'd failed many times. I think the problem was that I was focused on taking *out* a food group—like meat—but not on adding *in* the whole range of beautiful plant foods. I laugh now because every time I tell people I'm a vegan, they can't fathom how I could possibly feed myself. When I was on *The View*, the hosts asked me, "What do you eat?!" and I said, "Nothing! It's the easiest diet!"

But that couldn't be further from the truth. There's an abundance of foods available to you. This may come as a surprise, but lettuce and carrot sticks aren't the only plants out there. Beans, grains like barley, oats, and rice—they all grow out of the ground. These are plants too! And like vegetables, they have tons of disease-fighting, wellness-promoting nutrients and fiber that help keep things moving inside and out. To help get inspired about all the delicious options and ways to try them, I've included some of my favorite recipes in part 3. Flip through and see what looks good.

Now that you are structuring your diet from scratch and adding foods in one at a time, you have a chance to make eating work for you. Remember that this is a lifestyle, not a diet. It's eating to live, not eating to get by. The only rule is that you eat the foods that make you feel good and leave the ones that don't. Eat as many whole, plant-based foods as you want. There's no need to use a formula or a calorie count, because if you're being honest and listening to yourself, then you'll know what you need to eat and how much.

If you're still hesitant to take meat and dairy out of your diet, remember this: The more animal-based foods you eat, especially red meat, the worse it is for your health. And conversely, the fewer of these foods you eat, the greater the health benefits. And if you plan on eating them, then chances are when given the opportunity, you will. It's like trying to portion-control your heroin—eventually you're going to want to get high. Don't think of it as taking something away; think of it as having the freedom to eat all the plant-based foods you want. Fill up with these first and see if you still have an urge for meat and dairy. It's up to you how you want to improve your life; your state of well-being is *your* choice.

The Truth About Breakfast

One morning I got a call from Jody. She was about to end a twenty-one-day juice cleanse and transition into a plant-based diet, and she was frantic. "Robin, what can you eat for breakfast?!" It's been drilled into our minds that it's not breakfast without eggs, some toast, bacon and sausage, and maybe some pancakes. But that's just marketing. There's no rule against eating vegetables for breakfast! So I told her, every night when you go to sleep, guess what you do? You fast! You cleanse! And just as you don't want to dump a bunch of food in your still-groggy system after a detox, you don't want to do it in the morning either. I break my fast every morning with something light—some juice, maybe a piece of fruit, or a small plate of vegetables.

KNOW HOW YOUR FOOD GETS TO THE TABLE

If you're going to take the time to think about the food you're putting in your body, then you should also understand where it comes from in the first place. Most people couldn't tell you where their food was grown, the kind of soil it was grown in, whether it was sprayed down with pesticides, fungicides, and insecticides; or genetically modified. That's because it's confusing, and not entirely straightforward. It used to be that food was fairly simple—it went from the ground to a farmer's truck to the market. We could trust that the people growing our fruits and vegetables and grains weren't doing anything that could make us sick. But that's not necessarily the case anymore.

We assume that the government is protecting us, but the only thing they'll guarantee is "This won't kill you . . . today. You won't drop dead if you eat this. You may drop dead, but not today." Notice that the government gets upset only when someone becomes sick or dies and there's an undeniable connection to what they ate. You'll hear about E. coli or salmonella outbreaks, but what about the rising number of cases of cancer, diabetes, and heart disease? When it comes to our food supply, the government isn't telling us the whole truth.

Recently McDonald's, Burger King, and Taco Bell announced that they stopped using ammonium hydroxide in the production of their meat. This chemical, which is found in fertilizers, household cleaners, and even homemade explosives, is also used to "clean" undesirable beef scraps for human consumption. It will kill E. coli and other bacteria, but it also leaves unwanted residue in the "pink slime" that's then mixed with fillers and glommed into patties and tacos. But even though these few companies have come forward to say they'll no longer be slowly poisoning us with toxic beef, thanks to our trusty government, it's still a completely legal practice for every other meat manufacturer. The US Department of Agriculture classifies the chemical as "generally recognized as safe" and therefore *doesn't require any labeling on products that use it*. And what's more, it's estimated that pink slime constitutes at least 70 percent of our ground beef. The government and all its regulatory bodies that are supposed to be looking out for our health don't seem to mind that the food that you're feeding your family is robbing you of your health over the long term.

There is an overwhelming amount of evidence that most chronic diseases in America can be largely attributed to bad nutrition. Everyone from expert government panels to the surgeon general to academic scientists has agreed that more people die because of how they eat than by any other lifestyle or environmental factor, including tobacco use and car accidents. And yet the government is still supporting nutritional guidelines that tell us that so long as we're getting all the protein and carbohydrates that we need—regardless of whether that comes from a steak, a Froot Loop, or a carrot—we'll be in good shape. The problem is that there are companies who stand to lose a lot of money if Americans start thinking twice about the food they buy. McDonald's, Kraft Foods, the American Meat Institute, United Egg Producers, the National Dairy Council—these industry heavyweights have a big budget to defend their hold in our hunger economy, which conveniently funds some of the research that shapes our government's nutrition policies. Take, for instance, a panel for the Food and Nutrition Board that met to determine a safe upper limit on sugar and protein intake. They ultimately settled on 25 percent of one's diet as the magic number. But groups doing the same work in the international community settled on 10 percent. The difference? The FNB received funding from organizations like the Mars candy company and a group of soft-drink companies. The chair of the FNB had previously been a consultant to several major dairy-related companies or lobbies (the National Dairy Council, for example), and six of the eleven committee members also had ties to the industry. These guys aren't necessarily bad people—they're just trying to make a living. Groups like the National Dairy Council and the large-scale farms they represent—along with all the aforementioned heavyweights—have products to sell. So their efforts to get burgers into your hands and jugs of milk into your fridge aren't so you and your family can live happy, healthy lives. It's so they can make money! And all those millions of dollars that they're raking in are being put right back into the government's pockets through lobbying efforts.

We've lost a huge right when it comes to what we eat—and it's a pretty significant one. The quality of your food is just as important as the quality of your air and your water. But somehow the government got control over what's going into your body, and they're making decisions that favor industry over consumers. Or even decisions that don't seem to be doing much good for *anyone,* like allowing tomato paste on pizzas in school lunches to be counted as a vegetable. Who gave them the right? Each and every one of us has an obligation to get that back. It's your responsibility to figure out where your food comes from and what's happened to it—if anything—before it hits your table. The first step is to stop assuming that somebody out there cares so much about you that they're going to make sure your food supply is good and healthy. And the second is to never stop caring.

Right now we spend more time researching electronics, cars, furniture, and jewelry than we do our food. Is that a radiated stone? No, it's radiated fruit! They slap a lead apron on me at the dentist's office, and yet I'm eating this apple? Remember when milk used to go bad? Remember when bread used to mold? Now you can keep these things forever. What happened? What's in there? I was watching a sci-fi movie where the zombies figured out that if they eat food with as many preservatives as possible, they might live longer. We should be thinking the opposite. The same goes for hormones, pesticides, or any genes injected into our produce thanks to genetic engineering. I don't want fish genes in my corn! Like everything else we consume, it's "buyer beware." You have to be mindful of what it is exactly that you're purchasing. Here are a few rules to remember when shopping for food:

- **The only food that's not marketed to you is the good food:** People are always looking for buzzwords on processed foods when attempting good nutrition— "organic," "all natural," "fortified," etc. Forget it. The item in question might be made from something natural originally, it may have started in an organic field—tortilla chips might be made from organic corn—but natural? What's natural about a chip? I've never seen a tortilla tree! When you process something, you take everything that's good and natural and organic out of it. Then you have to attempt to stuff some synthetic vitamins and minerals back into it. Take a look at one of those labels. The fact that there's a list of ingredients should be the first red flag. What are the ingredients in an apple? In a bunch of carrots? There's no nutrition label on the kale. It is what it is. Even organic processed food has additives, so there's a good chance that whatever's in that box isn't going to give you what you need.

- Buy organic: Real, whole foods (read: actual fruits, vegetables, and grains) that are labeled 100 percent organic have the best nutritional pedigree. They're grown without chemical fertilizers; have little to no residue from synthetic pesticides or pharmaceuticals; aren't irradiated; and have higher levels of good-for-you antioxidants, flavonoids, vitamins, and minerals. And because the government doesn't deem it necessary to let you know whether bioengineers have tampered with your produce, the only way to guard yourself against genetically modified fruits and vegetables is to buy organic.

    Organic produce is better for your kids too. Standard chemicals used to process conventional produce are up to ten times more toxic to children than adults, and according to the Centers for Disease Control and Prevention, one of the main sources of pesticide exposure in kids comes from the food they eat. The U.S. Department of Health and Human Services says that one pesticide in particular—organophosphate pesticides (OP), which accounts for half of the insecticides used in the US—has been linked to hyperactivity, behavior disorders, learning disabilities, developmental delays, and motor dysfunction. More than four hundred chemicals and three hundred synthetic food additives are currently allowed to be used in conventional farming, but none are present in certified organic foods.

- Buy local: Just because you can get tomatoes from Mexico, grapes from Peru, and bananas from Guatemala doesn't mean you should. Schlepping these things over land, sea, and air takes a ton of fuel. In fact the food industry burns nearly a fifth of all the petroleum consumed in the US, which is about as much as cars do. And while growing organic food uses about a third less fossil fuel than doing it conventionally, industrial organic foods—those grown in large-scale operations and shipped around the country—can ultimately be *more* wasteful because keeping those cute little baby carrots cool and crisp for their cross-country road trip burns a lot of gas.

The solution is to buy food that is grown locally whenever you can. Your farmers market is one of the best resources for finding food that's not only grown responsibly but also doesn't have to travel too far. And when you're buying food from the people who have grown it, it takes all the guesswork out of whether it's good for you. Instead you'll get to fill up your basket with any number of beautiful, colorful fruits and vegetables harvested at the peak of their taste and nutritional quality. To find a market near you, go to www.ams.usda.gov and click on "Farmers Markets and Local Food Marketing."

REJOINING THE WORLD: EATING SOCIALLY

Just because you're eating a clean, plant-based diet doesn't mean that you'll be sentenced to monkish solitude or commune gatherings. Being social is an important part of life, and that includes going out to eat. But don't use eating out as an excuse to fall back into bad eating habits. I love eating in restaurants—it's like playing a game. I like to think of it as a puzzle that the waiter and the chef and I get to solve. I don't look at my dietary needs as a problem or as something to be embarrassed about. Attitude is everything. When I go out to eat, I'm expecting to have as good a time as everyone else; it's just a little different.

Once I was up in Boston and went to the restaurant in my hotel. They had a whole bunch of sides—Brussels sprouts, broccoli rabe, mushrooms—but of course they gunked them up with things like cheese sauce and breading. So when the waiter came over, I asked him how the vegetables were prepared *before* they got dunked in cholesterol. He said, "Well, we steam them." And I said, "Great! Just steam me a bunch of the vegetables and try to lay off the salt." And that was that. I got a big bowl of beautiful vegetables and could enjoy them knowing that there wasn't any other junk in there. Sometimes the simplest thing is what you want, though sometimes the kitchen will go the extra mile to whip up something special. So have fun with it! Tell your waiter exactly what your needs are and there's a good chance you'll end up with something the rest of the table will envy.

Every once in a while someone will ask if I want a bite off his or her plate. I just say, "No, thanks." I might think, *Oh, that looks so beautiful,* but then I go back to eating my own food. I'm not eyeing what everybody else has. I'm not trying to have somebody else's experience. You need to get past the idea that food is communal—it's not. Eating is personal. You're not having what your spouse is having or what your neighbor is having—*they're* eating it, and now their body is going to have to deal with it.

When Jody finished her first cleanse, she was so enthralled with how good she felt that I almost had to hold her ankles just to keep her from levitating. She was amazed by the transformation but also anxious about how she could continue to feel so good. "How do I hold on to this feeling?" she asked. "You have to fight for it," I said. "You can't just give in when you're with friends and someone says, 'Hey, let's order calamari for the table.'" You have to speak up—it's your body, your feeling, and your health. It might be hard for some people to understand because they're addicts and they don't want to lose members from their addict group. I'm always amazed when people actually care about what I'm eating. Sometimes I'll go out even when I'm detoxing and just have some tea or sneak a juice into my purse, and my friends will get upset and not want to eat. But I just say, "Please. I came because I want to be with you. And now I'll actually get to listen and not have my head stuck in a bowl." It's intimidating for some people, but just remind them that you're there for them, not for the food. Most of the time everyone's so busy eating that they've forgotten anyone else is at the table, and the conversation doesn't start up again because they're too exhausted digesting. I just look around and think, *Oh dear. Their eyes are closing. I guess it's time to go.*

I'm not saying it won't be difficult. It's hard to give up the foods you used to go to for fun or comfort. For me that was crab cakes. I grew up eating them—they were *it* for me. And some of the best crab cakes on earth are made on Long Beach Island, where I have my shore house. Now I can go out there and cook some up for visiting friends because I know that they're the best they'll have tasted. But I don't have any. They'll say, "Robin, I can't believe you don't want this." And to that I say, "I never want to feel the way I did." It's up to you to remember why you made this choice in the first place. Remember how crummy you used to feel and how much better you feel now. I guarantee that in time you'll start to look at those foods and wonder why you loved them so much in the first place. They weren't much solace when you could barely get out of bed in the morning!

8.

Be Good to Yourself

Being nice to yourself is tricky. In one sense, we're already way too nice. We're always indulging our taste buds, excusing ourselves from exercise, giving in to every whim and craving. We're really good at convincing ourselves that that extra cookie or hour of TV is going to offer some kind of relief from whatever it is that's really bothering us. But instead of asking, "Did it make me feel better?" we should be asking, "Did it nourish me?" Because chances are that after your five-minute sugar high wears off or *The Bachelor* is over, you'll be right back where you started. This isn't about what you need to take out of your life. This is about *adding* activities and practices that will help support your new, healthier lifestyle in a meaningful and enjoyable way. It's about self-love.

If you're disappointed in yourself or frustrated with your choices or unhappy with any part of your life, then you're most likely taking it out on your poor body. That's when you overindulge, whether with food or alcohol or drugs. The good news is that the path to self-love is fun and satisfying and it starts with how you take care of yourself. I have a friend who was suffering from cancer, and we talked about how she could very possibly have made decisions that helped that disease take root. I told her that now more than ever she needed to take care of her body like it's the most precious thing in the world. As soon as I said that, she took her arm and started kissing it, saying, "I'm so sorry!" We're not great at stopping to ask our bodies how they feel, or checking in to make sure everything's okay, that there's nothing they need. We just get up and go. But it's that checking in that builds self-love and, as a result, wellness. Because the time you spend on you is just as much a part of your health as what you're eating. You might not love your job and you may not have a lot of choice so that you can pay the bills, but when you do have time for yourself, make it count. Choose what's really important and, most of all, what makes you happy.

EAT FOR NUTRITION, NOT FOR ENTERTAINMENT

We're so quick to give ourselves that "special treat." *Oh, my boss was really mean to me; I deserve that slice of pizza* or *I had a hard day, so I'm going to be really good to myself and have that doughnut* or *Oh, I'm feeling down today; I'm going to treat myself to macaroni and cheese.* The first issue is that you're using food to avoid an issue. If you're eating because you're sad or lonely or upset, then figure out what it is that's making you sad or lonely or upset. The Häagen-Dazs isn't going to solve the problem for you. Start to notice when you reach for those treats and see if you can figure out a better way to cope with those feelings in a more direct, positive, productive way.

The second issue is that there's a disconnect between food and goodness. We should be treating ourselves with things that nourish us, things that really do make us feel better. Whether it's taking the time for a bubble bath, enjoying a walk, spending a half hour alone, or meditating, the important thing is to learn what really does make you feel better.

That said, food can still be fun. You can still have those special treats. But having something every day innately takes away its specialness. It's like riding a roller coaster. It might be something fun to do every once in a while, but you wouldn't do it every day.

Your regular life should be about sustaining, supporting, and nurturing yourself. But every once in a while, it's okay to indulge. It's okay to have a glass of wine every now and then—wine's a plant too!—but keep it special by not doing it every day.

GET MOVING

We used to get our exercise over the course of daily life, going out to hoe or dig or fish or hunt—all the things we had to do just to put dinner on the table. But now our food is sitting in a big freezer in the supermarket and all we have to do is get in a car, park as close as we can, use as few steps as possible to get in and out of the building, then go home and microwave it. So in light of that, we could at least get an hour of exercise, right? We need to replace all those things that we used to do to get our bodies moving. Because your body was meant to do it! And if you don't use it, you lose it. After my mother broke her ankle, I tried to convince her that the best thing she could do after it healed was start walking on it. But she never did, and now she has a frozen ankle. That's an entire body part that no longer works—and we get only one body in this lifetime. Sitting around has also been linked to all kinds of disease. The World Health Organization says that it's the cause for approximately 21–25 percent of breast and colon cancers, 27 percent of diabetes, and approximately 30 percent of heart disease cases.

Because I'd been so sick before all the detoxing, I had to first get myself well before I could even think about exercising. It had been a *long* time since I'd gotten any kind of regular physical activity, and I wasn't about to ask my body to reverse a year and a half of sitting around and eating the wrong stuff all in one go. But after a few months of giving my body the break it needed to heal and get stronger on its own, it actually told me that it was ready to get moving. I had more balance, I was more flexible, I had more stamina, and I was stronger—and that was merely with good nutrition! Just as all the mobility in my hand came back after surgery, all my body's faculties came back. I started going to the gym, lifting weights, and trying out new activities, like yoga.

Eventually I wanted to challenge myself more, so I found a running coach who taught me proper form and some basic stretches. We'd meet a few days a week in Central Park to do a little three-mile loop, but no matter how frequently we did it, I couldn't get past those three miles. I'd see other runners turning off the loop and onto a longer trail, and I'd think to myself, *I'm never going to do that. I don't know how to make myself do that!* But one day my trainer said, "You know, you really ought to give yourself a goal." And me being the ridiculous person that I am said, "Okay. I'll run a marathon."

Now, I'm not a runner. Yes, I was training to run the New York City Marathon, but it was *work*. There was no such thing as a runner's high for me. I had felt it *once* in my life and I figured if I was ever going to find it again, it would be training for the marathon. On the day of the race, Bobby Flay turned to me and said, "Robin, New York is going to put you on its shoulders and carry you through this race." Let me tell you something: I'm still waiting.

So maybe I'll never run another marathon, but it was an amazing experience and one that started just like any other journey—one step at a time. When I was twenty-eight and trying to get in shape so I wouldn't have to take a pill for the rest of my life, I decided to start a walking program, figuring I'd go out for a couple of miles every morning. So I went out the first day, and by the time I came home I just about fell through the door. My legs swelled up and I couldn't catch my breath. I had to buy old lady support hose just so I could help my blood pump back up to my heart while I slowly walked around the block every morning. But eventually I worked up to going farther and farther, and after a few months I started picking up the pace. I went from hobbling around the neighborhood in geriatric stockings to running three to five miles a day. You might have to start slowly, but the important thing is that you start.

Consider exercise another form of nourishment for your body. Think of it as *letting* your body do the things it naturally wants to do, not forcing it into something. Exercise doesn't have to mean torturing yourself with hours at the gym, running on the treadmill to nowhere. It can be any kind of motion that you enjoy. If dancing is something you like, find a way to add it to your life three or four times a week. If it's yoga, then go for it. Tennis, Rollerblading, running, horseback riding—whatever it is, find something that feels good, and do it enough to get the results that you want. If that's good muscle definition, good for you! If it's to run a certain number of miles, that's great! And if it's just to be healthy, then that's a noble goal too. Also think about adding more movement throughout the day. Experts now believe that just a single spurt of exercise isn't enough to consider yourself active. If you're on your butt all day—in a car, at a desk, on a couch— try to get ten minutes of activity for every hour you're sedentary. Walk around your office while on a call, get in gentle stretch during the morning news, or prop your computer monitor on a stack of books or a shelf and work standing up for a change. You'll feel more energized and productive.

LEARN TO RELAX

In my life, dealing with stress in a healthy way is a major priority. I'm constantly under pressure, and if I'm not careful, the silliest thing can set me off. I've had episodes where I'm standing in the middle of the office screaming because somebody took my umbrella. Finally some poor guy hands me his just so I'll get out of there!

When you eat a clean, plant-based diet you'll find that you feel less stressed in the first place because your mind is clearer and not so tangled up in dealing with your body's issues. And by the same token, you can take better care of your body when you're in a frame of mind to make good decisions. But no matter how many veggies you eat, you still need to find an outlet for the strain of everyday life.

Just as balance is crucial when it comes to our bodies and food, it's equally important in terms of our emotions. When we don't allow ourselves the space for quiet and relaxation, we upset our brain's balance. Normally the brain gets a signal that says, *Wait a minute. We're way too stressed out. Let's get out of our head for a moment.* But if you have a deadline or your child is crying or you're stuck in traffic, and you disregard the message that you need to relax? Now you have to go and do something that immediately releases that tension. For most people that usually means drinking too much, taking drugs, or overeating.

The key is to do something on a regular basis that recharges you. Have an outlet in your life that builds a reserve of cool and calm that you can draw upon when tension gets high. For me it's a hot bath. I have a whole routine where every evening I turn off my phone and soak for twenty minutes, completely undisturbed. It makes life that much more bearable. Some people get a massage or other kinds of bodywork, like acupuncture or Reiki. Some people meditate or have a spiritual practice. Others find reading or being in nature relaxing. You don't have to limit it to just one activity, and it certainly doesn't have to be intellectual. Sometimes I zone out in front of the TV. I watch something that has nothing to do with anything, and I just melt into it before I go to bed. Then I can say I've had some time for me to just entertain myself and indulge a naughty pleasure. It doesn't have to be a huge investment. Just fifteen to twenty minutes of "me time" on a regular basis makes emotional extremes a lot easier to handle.

Shut Up and Listen!

Just as you can listen to what your body wants you to feed it, you can also tune in to whether your body needs a little extra care. Most people assume that when they start to feel sick—sore throat, runny nose, lack of energy—"there's something going around." So they take an antihistamine or cold medication and keep going. Or they try to avoid getting sick by slathering themselves with Purell. I remember running into a friend at Staples, and she had a case of the stuff in her cart.

"I'm getting ready for bird flu," she said. "What are you going to do??"

"Not get it!"

When it comes to getting sick, we've come to feel like complete victims of our environment—like we don't have this incredible immune system that has the ability to protect us, so long as we take care of it. When I get sick, it's not because there's a cold virus army conspiring to attack me—it's because I made myself vulnerable. I didn't give my immune system enough material to make white blood cells and antibodies, and so the defenses were down. But if you listen to those early warning signs, you can give your system what it needs to fend off foreign invaders. When I start to feel sluggish or achy or a cold coming on, that's my body telling me that it needs a boost. I stop whatever I'm doing, get some sleep, slug down some green juice, and let my body take it from there.

SURROUND YOURSELF WITH PEOPLE YOU ACTUALLY LIKE

How much of your life is about enduring or surviving the people in it? So many of the things we do are about impressing other people or making them happy and have very little to do with our actual wants and needs. Have you ever really looked at the quality of the people in your life? Are your friends truly your friends? Is your family truly support-ive? Do you truly enjoy being around them? As I said before, you don't always have a lot of choice when it comes to your time. We have an abundance of obligations that dictate how we spend our day. So when it comes to the time that's actually yours, make sure you're spending it with people who love you and treat you well. The people you need to have a drink to be with or eat junk food to be with or take a pill to be with? You don't need them. And if they can't understand, support, and respect the new choices you're making in your life, then you especially don't need them. You can't control everything in your life, but you can control whom you spend your time with. Well, for the most part—there are holidays. But the times when you do get to choose, choose what's best for you.

GET SOME SLEEP

Sleep is a crucial part of taking better care of yourself. There are countless studies that show that people who don't get enough sleep have a tendency to be overweight and are more adversely affected by stress. And yet we make sleep such a low priority. We admire the man who says he needs only four hours of sleep. But look at him? Do you really want to be him? If it meant you were fat, tired, and sick, would you still want to be him? You need to get more sleep, and you need to get *better* sleep.

High-quality sleep is uninterrupted, in a dark room, and it's deep. You're not tossing and turning and waking up several times a night and then not going back to sleep. It's not falling asleep with the TV on. It's not taking a pill to fall asleep. That is not the kind of sleep we're talking about. You might as well just stay up. Sleep should be one of the most enjoyable things you do. You should look at your bed and say, "I can't wait to get to you!"

If you look at your bed and think, *Oh no!,* you've got a problem. And you should get it resolved, because it's killing you.

As for an amount of sleep to aim for, get as much deep, sound shut-eye as you can. You should wake up in the morning with a sense of rest and wellness. If that means you need eight hours, then make sure you get eight hours. If you need more, then that's okay too. Researchers have discovered that eight hours isn't necessarily the standard and that we should aim to get what we need to feel rested. Just know that you can't make up for missed sleep on a minute-to-minute basis. If you miss an hour, you can't simply nap for an hour to feel caught up. And if you sleep for ten hours, you can't bank the extra two for a rainy day. Get the sleep you need and make it good.

DO SOMETHING MEANINGFUL

After you've cleared away some of the noise of your body's aches and pains and alleviated the stress of daily life, you should think about filling that space with meaningful activity. Consider doing something every day that makes your heart and soul feel good—and not something like going to work or exercising or feeding yourself—something that gives back too. Because if you have the wealth of health, then you ought to be contributing. It doesn't have to be feeding the children of Africa or adopting twenty orphans; it can be as simple as watching the kids while your partner reads a book or using some of your new recipes to make dinner for your neighbor. See what contributing positively does for your life; you may be surprised.

FIND A DOCTOR WHO HELPS

Remember back in chapter 3 when I told you that your doctor might not know how to treat the whole body instead of its individual pieces? Well, here's the part where you do something about it. If you're going to take control of your health, then you need to form a relationship with a health practitioner who not only understands your specific needs but can monitor things like your hormones, vitamins, nutrients, and cholesterol; screen you for disease; and provide counsel for the mental, emotional, and spiritual aspects of your life. It's what's called *functional medicine*. Most physicians practice an acute-care approach—or what I like to call a pill-per-problem approach. They'll address immediate problems or symptoms, but they often don't look at the underlying causes. So you end up with a lot of pills *and* a lot of problems. Functional medicine practitioners, on the other hand, look at the body and its systems as a whole. They're not just looking at you as a cardiologist or hematologist or endocrinologist—they're looking at *everything*. Because you can't find any sustainable solutions to your health in a vacuum.

And what's even more significant, proponents of functional medicine focus not on what's wrong but on how to keep things *right*. Wellness isn't the absence of disease; it's prevention through nutrition, diet, and exercise. To find a physician or other type of practitioner trained in functional medicine, go to http://functionalmedicine.org. Whether you choose to work with a practitioner from this site, a friend's recommendation, or an insurance company referral, there are steps you can take to make sure that he or she is the right fit:

- Ask how much time you'll get in his or her office: The key is forming a *relationship* with this person. Would you ever want to be in a relationship with someone who made you wait for an hour, then spent fifteen minutes feeling you up before hurrying to see her next prospect? No! So why accept that from your doctor? You want to find a practitioner who is going to spend time with you. Call the office and ask. Ideally you would get an hour for a first meeting and a follow-up. Once you've done any testing and have a treatment plan in place, then a fifteen-minute appointment should be appropriate.

  Another option is to ask if the doctor might be willing to chat briefly about your particular health concerns. Offer to pay for her time, since she is most likely calling on her lunch break or during time she might otherwise be spending with patients. Believe me, by figuring out before your visit whether you and the doctor are on the same page, you'll save a ton of money in the long run for just a little up front. That said, doctors are extremely busy, and more often than not they'll ask that you just go ahead and book an appointment, but it never hurts to ask.

- Ask what the doctor's specialty or passion is: While well versed in total care, practitioners can still have special interests or expertise in particular kinds of health. If you have more specific concerns than general maintenance, then it's appropriate to ask whether it's an area that particular doctor is keen to navigate. You want to work with someone as passionate about your needs as you are.

- Ask if the doctor accepts insurance: The one downside to working with physicians trained in functional medicine is that there's a higher likelihood that they don't accept insurance. It's not because they're dealing in some shady back-alley operation, it's because the insurance model is miserably outdated. The companies require doctors to use codes—much like the Dewey decimal system—for their diagnoses and treatments. But oftentimes the codes either don't match what is *actually* wrong with you or fail to sum up an appropriate treatment, i.e., "the patient has high blood pressure and received a prescription for Sectral" versus "the patient has elevated blood pressure caused by stress and received a treatment plan of acupuncture and fewer animal foods." And because your doctor should prefer to spend her time with you and not arm-wrestling insurance companies, this might be his or her arrangement.

  That said, there's a good chance that your insurance company will reimburse you for the visits. Find out beforehand what the set-up will be, both between you and the doctor and between you and the insurance company, and whether coverage will include lab tests.

- Consider whether you actually *like* this person: Your doctor should be someone you can talk to, someone you trust, someone you feel genuinely cares about you and your health, and, most of all, someone you want to see. For a long time, I cut doctors out of the equation because I had so many bad run-ins. What I missed out on were all the screenings that could have caught the growing mass in my pelvis. Now I know how invaluable it is to have a relationship with a doctor who is going to be my partner and advocate.

What Are You Saving For?

The most common excuse I hear about not seeing an out-of-network doctor or requesting extra blood work—or buying organic food, for that matter—is that it's more expensive. But I don't hear those same excuses when it comes to springing for kids' sneakers or iPods or the latest had-to-haves. We're scrimping pennies in the wrong places. Right now we're paying an exorbitant amount of money for the kind of care where we still don't really know what's wrong with us or how to get better. We're spending entire paychecks for pills and doctor visits that will only lead to more pills and doctor visits yet paying pocket change for the food that's supposed to keep us healthy. We'd rather scrimp on personalized care, crucial blood tests, and healthy whole foods so we can have $100,000 operations covered by insurance. But there's a risk in all this and it's not just the gamble you take every time you introduce a new chemical into your body or undergo anesthesia. It's that your health care is the difference between high-quality life and death, and right now you're putting money into the pockets of people who don't have enough interest in the former and are only moving you closer to the latter.

An Ounce of Prevention Is Worth a Pound of Cure: How Blood Tests Can Save Your Life

Blood tests are crucial when it comes to getting an accurate picture of your overall health. Understanding exactly what's going on in your body is necessary for your doctor to care for you appropriately, but unfortunately the current standard blood panels are completely out of date and are leading doctors to overmedicate their patients. Take your traditional cholesterol test: You've probably been tested and know your "number," but that's only half the story. Cholesterol comes in two sizes—there's the big particles, or HDL, and the small, LDL. As we talked about before, LDL are the sticky little bastards that like to cling to our arteries and ruin things for everyone. HDL, on the other hand, are actually absorbent and can help ferry some of these LDL particles back to the liver for reprocessing. But if your cholesterol test is only counting the total particles, then your doctor has no way of knowing whether you're stocked up with useful HDL or clogged to the gills with LDL. And if he sees a number he doesn't like, you could end up on medication when a change in diet, additional exercise, and some extra niacin and fish oil would have done the trick. These medications, or statins—the most widely prescribed drug in the world—come with a host of their own issues. They've been linked to memory loss and diabetes, as well as muscle pain and leg spasms that are exacerbated by exercise. (So you can forget trying to get your cholesterol in check the good ol' fashioned way!)

The point I'm trying to make is that the more accurate information you have about your health, the better both you and your doctor can *maintain and improve* your well-being. The tests listed below are a good place to start for assessing your general picture of wellness and will allow a health care practitioner to tailor a plan of action to your needs. Requesting lab tests can sometimes mean having to pay out-of-pocket, but remember what I said about where we're scrimping? Wouldn't you rather find a way to pay for blood work now than a lifetime of medication and surgeries?

THE BLOOD TEST MENU

Chemistry Panel and Complete Blood Count (CBC)

Vitamin D

Vitamin B_{12}

Ferritin

Fasting Insulin

ee T3, Free T4, and Thyroid Antibodies

PART THREE

RECIPES AND KITCHEN KNOW-HOW

9.

The Joy of Cooking

So there I was, a new vegan, basically surviving on salads and juice. I would have preferred some variety, but I had no idea where to start. I'd sometimes go out to eat, but too often the only menu option available was some steamed vegetables drowning in oil and salt. I figured that most chefs couldn't imagine someone who *wanted* to eat just vegetables. It finally occurred to me that if I was going to get exactly what I wanted to eat, I was going to have to make it myself.

At that point in my life, the kitchen was a foreign place. One time I tried to boil water and came back ten minutes later to find I'd burned a hole through one of the other empty pots on the range. I'd turned the wrong burner on. Then there was the time I attempted to cook a steak. I'd never used the oven in my apartment before, but I'd heard about people using the broiler for meat. So I turned the oven on, threw the steak into what I thought was the broiler—without seasoning it or marinating it because I didn't know about any of that stuff—and went in the other room to read. About ten minutes later I came back in to check on it, figuring it shouldn't take too long, but the steak was still raw. And cold. I just figured I had a slow broiler. So I went back to what I was doing, and five minutes later I checked it again. Nothing. Ten minutes later, nothing. I finally opened the oven door, saw that the broiler thing was all lit up, and realized: The steak was in a drawer. That's how *not* a cook I was.

But when I was on vacation in Sedona and couldn't find anything I wanted to eat, I thought maybe I'd give this cooking thing a try. I resolved to go out and get some vegetables, take them back to my little kitchenette, and experiment. I bought some ingredients that I recognized—Brussels sprouts and mushrooms—threw them in a pan with a little bit of oil, cooked them until they smelled good, and gave the concoction a taste. It was good! Before then the only Brussels sprouts I'd had were the mushy beige things I ate growing up. But these had a nice brown caramelly thing going on. I thought, *Wow, I could do this with any other vegetables.* I realized that if I started cooking, I'd not only know what I was eating—because in a restaurant you never know how much salt or oil or butter they've added to things—I'd be able to make *exactly* what I wanted. Before long I had a solid repertoire of dishes to choose from because I felt confident enough to play with new ingredients, spices, and cooking methods.

I love what cooking has brought to my life. I'm still not what you'd consider to be a master chef, but for me it's not about doing things perfectly. It's about getting in the kitchen, embracing the adventure, and relishing every last bite. Working with Christopher Sanchez, of the amazing Black Eyed Susans Cafe, a chef with the supreme gift of giving vegetables their delicious due, I've put together some of my favorite recipes, which finally make the healthy stuff king. We're so used to thinking of vegetables like medicine—hold your nose and take your vegetables! They were the yucky gray mush relegated to the side of the plate. Meanwhile we had it drilled into our heads that meat should be the main attraction.

These dishes are testament to how filling and extraordinarily delicious things like vegetables, beans, legumes, and grains can be. There's nothing "health food" about them. When the ingredients you're using are fresh and packed with vibrant goodness, you'll see how complex and deeply satisfying they can be. All the sensations you love about food—crunchy, earthy, meaty, creamy, tangy, crispy—are all right here. In fact many of these recipes are inspired by food I used to love. Take the Eggplant or Asparagus "Takeout" with Chinese Garlic Sauce (page 170)—that was my to-go go-to. It was basi-

cally vegetables bathed in oil, sugar, and MSG. Talk about a trifecta! After playing around in the kitchen with Chris, though, we were able to re-create that sweet-and-spicy, garlicky sauce that not only hits the spot but also lets the vegetables do some of the talking.

Howard sometimes orders in vegetarian meals for lunch, and there are days when you can't tell what's what in all that green-brown mush. "I think that's what 'vegetarian' means," he said when I asked him about it. "That you can't recognize your food." I, obviously, beg to differ. The recipes you'll find here are my love letters to vegetables. You'll find all kinds of delectable treatments of my earth-grown friends, and they have the same thing in common: You can taste the veg! These recipes aren't about tricking you into liking vegetables; they're to showcase just how incredible these natural flavors can be with a little help from a few simple ingredients. Brussels sprouts sautéed until they're crispy and golden, then coated in creamy miso dressing, isn't a throwaway side dish; it's the star dish! An eggplant that's been roasted with fresh herbs and olive oil until it's caramelized and custardy isn't just a vegetable anymore—it's *indulgent*. Throw on a pot of brown rice or other whole grain, and you have dinner.

I've also included two menus for special occasions, because if there is one thing that I associate with celebrations and holidays, it's food. When I started to change my diet, I was worried that I might not be able to enjoy myself as much at parties and gatherings if I couldn't partake in all the dishes that I'd come to associate with having a good time. But the more I experienced the world of eating plants—and especially the more I cooked— the more I realized just how sumptuous and special and exquisitely delicious these foods can be.

But in case you're STILL not sold, here are *my* favorite reasons for cooking:

- It's better for you. Preparing your own food is the only way to know *exactly* what you're putting in your body. Restaurant food and food in packages are minefields of hidden ingredients, like additives, sugar, and salt. That's why I cook—who needs to be reading and reading and reading a label just to eat? You need to know how nutritious your food is the same way you need to know that your water and air are clean—you're building your body out of it. You wouldn't drink out of a puddle just because you're thirsty, right? But that's essentially what we do with food. We opt for bottled water over tap if there's any doubt in our minds that it could make us sick, but we're playing Russian roulette with what we eat. We let somebody else make it—whether it's Taco Bell, Applebee's, Kellogg's, or the chef at the fancy restaurant, and we never ask, "Is this good for me? Is this what I need?" When you cook your own food, you take away all the guesswork and unnecessary junk.
- It's not that hard! One night not too long ago, I was invited to a small get-together a friend was hosting. She had a tiny Manhattan kitchen and asked if I'd bring some of the food. I gladly agreed—then got too busy to do any of the cooking until 4:30 that afternoon. I raced home with groceries and was able to whip up four gorgeous dishes (Wild Mushroom Risotto [page 196], Swiss Chard

with Cocount Curry [page 166] Marrakesh-Blend Squash Soup [page 126], and Spicy Roasted Cauliflower with Pimenton [page 168]), grab my homemade Pickled Vegetables [page 172] from the fridge, and be in the car by 6:30 p.m.

The reaction I got when everyone saw the spread? "Who catered?" They couldn't believe that not only could I make all this but that it was so *good*. Everyone was amazed by how you could taste each vegetable's unique flavor, and because the food wasn't bogged down with heavy oil or salt, they all ran back for seconds.

I've come a long way from sticking steaks in drawers, but I'm still proof that you too can tackle these recipes. Perhaps like you, when I first began cooking I was starting from scratch. Everything was foreign to me, and I used the wrong utensils all the time. I thought you were supposed to use a tiny paring knife to cut vegetables, and it would always take *forever*. Then I realized that real chefs were using a great big knife to cut their vegetables, even little things like garlic, and I thought, *Oh, that looks scary—but it's definitely a quicker way to do it!* I was afraid of heat, so my pan was never hot enough to cook in. Not anymore—give me a bonfire! I was afraid of the grill because of the scary-looking open flames, but now it's one of my favorite ways to cook. I'll show you how just a few basic tools, techniques, and staples can completely change your outlook on cooking.

• **Cooking brings people together.** My favorite thing by far about cooking is that it's so communal. People make a big deal about eating together and the family meal, but people should be *cooking* together. It's a fun way to spend time with your family, and then everyone wants to try the food they had a hand in making. Want to know the best way to get your kids eating vegetables? Let them help prep. When they see the kale leaves they tore up wilt into some creamy beans or the zucchini ribbons they helped make getting tossed in vinaigrette, I guarantee they're going to want to see what those ingredients taste like.

And cooking is the perfect way to celebrate, even when there's no special occasion. At my house in the summer, it's everybody's responsibility to cook and help set the table and do whatever it takes to get that meal ready. The best part is sitting down and enjoying something that we all made together. Before I would usually just sit around until the meal was served, saying, "I can be a good taster!" Meanwhile everyone would be in the kitchen having a good time. Now I love being in my kitchen, talking and laughing about everything and anything, and feeling the absolute joy in providing that for other people.

Kids and Food: Ending the Battle with Vegetables

If there's one thing parents say that makes me crazy, it's this: "My kid hates vegetables." They say that *they* have no problem changing the way they eat, but it's their kids who will be the problem. Well, guess what? They have it backward. Being healthy is a natural inclination—we're not born craving Cheez-Its and M&M's. We're *introduced* to these foods. Your kids don't hate vegetables because it's some universal rule; your kids hate vegetables because they've never been exposed to them in an appealing way.

Most of the time dinner is a war. Kids are told they have to sit down and clean their plates, regardless of whether they're hungry. You threaten them so they'll eat that tasteless stalk of whatever sitting next to their macaroni and cheese, and you wonder why they hate vegetables! Don't you remember going through that yourself? I sure do! Vegetables were always getting me stuck at the table.

To get your kids eating healthy foods, start with not forcing them to eat anything. No one ever starved in a house full of food. Let them eat when they get hungry, and when they do, give them good choices. I promise that if all you're putting out is carrots and some hummus, your kids—if they're hungry—will eat carrots and some hummus.

Which leads me to my second point: When you celebrate fresh, whole foods the same way you would chicken fingers or pizza, kids pay attention. I have friends who made a concerted effort to expose their kids to fruits and vegetables from day one. They were at a party and a guy asked the kids to choose between candy and apples. When the kids chose apples, the guy turned to my friends and said, "You've brainwashed your children." To that I say, "Well, why not?!" Instead of brainwashing your kids to eat junk, why not brainwash them into the good stuff? I'm not saying that your children need to sit alone in the corner at birthday parties while the other kids have cake, but what you eat at home teaches your kids how to think about food so they'll make smart decisions everywhere else. And if you trust your kids to make those decisions outside the home, then there's a good chance they'll do you proud.

Aside from cooking with kids, which is really the best way to get them excited about new foods, try planning an outing to an organic farm or farmers market. I don't mean just an apple orchard or pumpkin patch in the fall; I'm talking about going to visit where all their fruits and vegetables come from. They can see how the plants grow out of the ground, how the farmer harvests them, and what it looks like when someone is taking good care of their land. At a farmers market they can discover the fascinating variety of fruits and vegetables that are out there and meet some of the interesting people who grow their food. It's a great way to get out and enjoy nature, to learn something with your child, and to involve the rest of the family when you go home and cook your finds for dinner.

10.

Getting Started

Think of getting back into the kitchen as an adventure. You're going to discover new ingredients, new flavors, new techniques, and a newfound sense of accomplishment. To get you from here to there, however, there are a few tools you'll need.

GEAR UP

The first tools you'll need are actual ones—like knives and bowls and measuring spoons. Before you rush out to Williams-Sonoma to outfit your kitchen from soup to nuts, know that you really only need a few basic items to create most of these recipes. You don't need a whole rack of fancy pots and pans, and you definitely don't need a knife for every task—you're not a surgeon! The essentials include: one good knife, a cutting board, measuring cups and spoons, tongs, two large mixing spoons, a colander, a baking sheet, and two or three good pots and pans. For a more detailed list of items that will come in handy as you work your way through this book, see appendix A.

TALK TO YOUR GROCER/FARMER/ FARMERS MARKET ATTENDANT

There are going to be ingredients in these recipes that you've never heard of—don't worry about it! I still wander around my grocery store confused. When I was shopping for some of the recipes for this book, I needed celery root. I had no *idea* what a celery root looked like. But I found my produce guy, asked him about it, and he pointed me in the right direction. Believe it or not, ladies and gentlemen, the man didn't judge me for not knowing what a celery root was.

When I first started cooking, there were some ingredients that I was too intimidated to pick up because I'd never used them before. But then I got braver. I started bringing home coconuts. I couldn't figure out how to get into the darn things—bashing them on the driveway sure wasn't working—and so I *asked*. I realized that the men and women growing my food or getting it to me fresh were the resources I'd been missing. They know what's in season, what's tasting good, and whether you roast, sauté, grill, broil, or steam it. And now that you'll have all these new cooking skills under your belt, you'll know exactly what to do when you go home. Whatever you do, don't expect to learn everything from this book. Don't get me wrong—it's a good start—but it's not the final word on vegetables. This is a starting point for you to go and find out what else is in the wide world of vegetables. Then come back to *me* with suggestions!

HAVE SOME FUN

After I got back from Sedona with newfound kitchen confidence, I started getting inspired. I'd see what they were doing in restaurants and think, *What was in that salad?* Oh, fennel! I'm going to go find some fennel. Or leeks, I gotta go find those because they were really good. And I'd just throw them in my skillet. And I discovered that I didn't even mind if something was only partially successful because I was making the effort to do something nice for myself.

Then I'd watch cooking shows and realize that I wanted to learn more about spices. So one night I made soup for a friend and threw in whatever I had in the cabinet. Mrs. Dash maybe? Some dried oregano? God knows what was in there, but you know what? It turned out great! Spices and herbs are what flavor everything you eat. No one just gets a steak, throws it into the pan, then eats it. They marinate the darn thing for hours, then pound it and poke holes in it and shove things in it and sprinkle things on it. The flavor comes from the combination of the meat and spices. I learned that if I used the flavors that reminded me of my favorite dishes, it would create the same sensation. I loved lamb cooked with rosemary, so I bought fresh rosemary, chopped it up, and threw it in with some roasted purple potatoes. It was delicious! Meaty and toasty brown and perfumed by the herbs. It was everything that lamb could offer me, without all the torture on my system.

In appendix D, I put together a list of spices and herbs commonly found in cuisines such as Asian, Indian, Greek, Italian, and French. Think you'll miss nachos, with all that grease and congealed cheese? You'd be amazed at what a little cumin, cayenne pepper, and cilantro can do to a bowl of black beans.

Playing around with herbs and spices is also one of the easiest ways to take plain old sautéed vegetables and turn them into a satiating meal. (For my favorite example, take a look at Orange and Ginger–Glazed Carrots on page 147.) Experiment with fresh herbs and dried, and for a more intense flavor from your spices, try toasting them in a dry pan over medium-high heat. They're done when they're fragrant, which usually takes just a minute or two.

PLAN AHEAD

Don't get overwhelmed with all the dishes you'd like to try. Select a few for the week, plot out your plan of attack, and, above all else, *make a shopping list*. The first few trips to the store might be daunting because of all the new ingredients in your cart, but if you keep up the cooking, you'll find that they're used again and again.

In order to save myself time during the week, I like to do a lot of my cooking on the weekend, then store meals in the freezer and fridge. Include a couple of the dressings or sauces, and you'll make quick work of your farmers market haul. If you'd prefer to cook throughout the week, save yourself time by prepping and washing vegetables before you store them in the fridge.

11.

Recipes

A Note on Ingredients

There are several ingredients that make an appearance in almost all of these recipes and, for that reason, call for having the best product possible.

Soy sauce: This Asian condiment is one of the easiest ways to add a lot of flavor to a dish instead of salt. That said, you'll want to choose a brand that is low-sodium and doesn't contain added sugar. You can also substitute Bragg Liquid Aminos, which uses only non-GMO (non–genetically modified organism) soybeans.

Olive oil: I use good-quality extra-virgin olive oil in all my preparations. You'll want to be using a brand with a flavor you like, especially when you're drizzling it over uncooked items like salads. Try a few to see what you prefer—spicy, fruity, mild, etc.

Produce: Unless noted, use fresh. Frozen fruits and vegetables can be okay in the winter, but you'll get the best results using ingredients that are in season.

Salt: In all cases, these recipes call for kosher salt.

Don't Commit a Salt and Battery

When you're cooking to bring out the truest flavor of an ingredient, you don't need a lot of salt. Salt is there to enhance the taste of whatever you're cooking, not to undermine it. Accordingly, we've meticulously found ways to add as little as possible. Don't be tempted to go dumping more in. You can't fool around with salt. You put in one grain too many and your dish goes from perfect to salty. So do me a favor and taste your food first before you go messing with it. If you're using these recipes, there's a very good chance you won't need to alter them.

If you are on a low-salt diet, feel free to omit the salt entirely. Because of all the spices and herbs in each dish, eliminating it won't change the flavor dramatically.

JUICES

Juice is the ultimate nutrient delivery system—it's essentially mainlining vegetables. Juices are a delicious and convenient way to get a highly concentrated dose of all-things-good-for-you. Just don't OD with food *and* juice: Because they're so nutrient-dense, juices are meals in a cup.

Feel free to adjust these recipes to your own tastes. If one is too "green" for you, try adding a bit more lemon or ginger.

If you're following the Master Class Juice Cleanse, all of these recipes—with the exception of the Carrot, Apple, Ginger Juice (page 113)—can be on your menu.

Apple, Fennel, Kale Juice

MAKES 1 JUICE

1 apple, cored
¼ bulb fennel
½ cucumber
¼ lemon, peeled
2 large kale leaves
½-inch piece fresh ginger
1 stalk celery
2 large romaine leaves

Pass all the ingredients through a juicer.

Cucumber, Celery, Spinach Juice

MAKES 1 JUICE

1 large cucumber
3 stalks celery
2 handfuls spinach
2 large romaine leaves
1 tablespoon fresh parsley leaves

Pass all the ingredients through a juicer.

Green Leaf Juice

2 cups spinach

3 Swiss chard leaves

2 romaine leaves

¼ lemon, peeled

Pass all the ingredients through a juicer.

Carrot, Apple, Ginger Juice

1 pound carrots, ends trimmed

1 green apple, cored

1-inch piece fresh ginger

Pass all the ingredients through a juicer.

SMOOTHIES

Smoothies are the milk shakes of the vegan world. What I like the best is that, unlike juices, you're not losing any of the fiber goodness of the fruits (and some vegetables). And it doesn't hurt that they're bright, cold, sweet, and decadently creamy. I love making a smoothie with kids and letting them guess what color it's going to be—then letting them gobble it down like ice cream. Just remember: It's not a smoothie without a straw!

These recipes all stand on their own as meals and can be tailored to your tastes by substituting in other fruits or other liquids, like coconut water, hemp milk, or soymilk, to adjust the consistency.

Peach Almond-Butter Smoothie

MAKES 1 SMOOTHIE

1½ cups almond milk

1 cardamom pod

1½ cups peeled and sliced peaches, fresh or frozen

1 cup diced mango, fresh or frozen

½ banana

¼ cup almond butter

⅔ cup ice

In a small pot, heat roughly 2 tablespoons of the almond milk and the cardamom pod until just warm. Let steep for 20 minutes. Discard the cardamom pod.

Place all of the almond milk and the remaining ingredients in a blender and process until smooth.

CHEF'S NOTE:
THE MANGO

To get the most flesh out of a mango, stand the fruit vertically and picture a large oval seed inside that runs from top to bottom. Insert the tip of your knife to find it, then run your knife down its sides to remove the "cheeks." Place the cheeks skin-side down on your cutting board and, again using the tip of your knife, gently score the flesh in a grid pattern, trying not to cut through the skin. Pick up a cheek, flip it inside out, and run your knife along the skin to remove the little squares.

Avocado, Pineapple, Chili, Lime Smoothie

MAKES 1 SMOOTHIE

½ avocado, peeled and pitted
2 cups diced fresh pineapple
¼ jalapeño, seeds removed and coarsely chopped
½ teaspoon fresh lime juice
¼ cup coconut water

Place all the ingredients in a blender and process until smooth.

Green Smoothie

MAKES 1 SMOOTHIE

½ cup almond milk
2 kale leaves
1 banana
½ cup ice

Place the almond milk and kale in a blender and process until smooth.
Add the banana and ice and blend until smooth.

SOUPS

Detox Soup and Broth

For an easy way to boost the vegetable quotient during your cleanse—whether you're taking baby steps, going all-veg, or jumping headfirst into the Master Class—make a big pot of detox soup to have for dinner. You can use the basic format of any of the soups listed in this section, especially the Silky Broccoli Soup (page 119), "Cream" of Cauliflower Soup (page 120), and Hearty Greens Soup with Farro (page 122). Just make a few adjustments. Omit any salt and pepper; avoid starchier vegetables, such as butternut squash or corn, and night-shades, such as tomatoes, peppers, and eggplant; and steer clear of spicy ingredients like chili peppers, paprika, and cayenne. (And leave out the farro in the Hearty Greens Soup.) Leafy greens are a cleanser's best friend, so incorporate as many as you can. Feel free to get creative with fresh herbs like thyme, sage, and rosemary; with dried herbs and spices like oregano, turmeric, and basil; or by adding a spritz of fresh lemon juice. Just because it's a detox doesn't mean it has to be bland.

If you're juice cleansing, I highly recommend making a batch of Mushroom Consommé (page 123), omitting the salt and pepper, to sip throughout the day.

Free-Form Vegetable Stock/Broth

PREP TIME: 10 MINUTES   **COOK TIME:** 20 TO 30 MINUTES

I highly recommend making a big batch of this simple broth. It stores well in the freezer and adds an instant pick-me-up to almost all the recipes in this book when substituted for water. It also works really nicely as a detox broth if you omit the seasonings. In either case, you can use any mixture of mild-flavored vegetables, including any scraps or peels you might have left over from cooking. Just steer clear of overpowering varieties like turnips or harsh, bitter greens.

Any mixture of mild-tasting vegetables, such as leeks, celery, carrots, fennel, including scraps and peels. No turnip or harsh-tasting green vegetables.
1 bay leaf
Pinch of coriander seeds
Pinch of black peppercorns
Handful of herbs such as thyme or parsley

Add the vegetables to a large soup pot, coarsely chopping any that aren't already. Cover with double their volume of cold water, add herbs and spices, and bring to a simmer over medium-high heat. Allow to simmer for 20 to 30 minutes. Strain and serve or store.

Silky Broccoli Soup

PREP TIME: 20 MINUTES   **COOK TIME:** 15 MINUTES
SERVES 10

Unlike heavy, cream-based soups, this version of cream of broccoli gets its body and flavor from using all the edible parts of the vegetable. The result is a pure, bright broccoli flavor in a silky soup that's perfect as a lighter spring dish.

1 tablespoon olive oil

2 cloves garlic, sliced

1 cup finely diced white onion

1 teaspoon fennel seeds

1 bay leaf

1 head broccoli, separated into medium-size florets, stems cut into
   ¼-inch-thick slices

1 teaspoon salt

½ teaspoon black pepper

Pinch of red pepper flakes

6 cups low-sodium vegetable stock or water

In a large pot, heat the oil over medium heat. Add the garlic, onion, fennel seeds, bay leaf, and broccoli stems and sauté for 3 to 4 minutes, until the onion becomes translucent. Add the florets, salt, black pepper, red pepper flakes, and enough stock or water to cover the vegetables by about 2 inches. Bring to a boil, reduce to a simmer, and cook until the stems become tender, 8 to 10 minutes. Remove from the heat, discard the bay leaf, and puree the soup in batches. Adjust the consistency as desired with stock or water.

For an optional garnish, reserve 1 cup of the florets and toss them with ¼ teaspoon salt, ¼ teaspoon black pepper, a pinch of red pepper flakes, and 1 tablespoon olive oil, then roast in a 400°F oven for 20 minutes, or until tender and crunchy.

"Cream" of Cauliflower Soup

PREP TIME: 1 HOUR OR OVERNIGHT   **COOK TIME:** 35 MINUTES

SERVES 10

Something magical happens when you puree cashews—they have the sweet, rich taste and consistency of cream. Add them to soup with some meaty, nutty cauliflower and you get the warm bowl of soul-soothing goodness that you just need on a chilly afternoon.

2 cups raw cashews

6 cups water or low-sodium vegetable stock

2 tablespoons olive oil

1 cup coarsely chopped, well-washed leeks

1 celery heart, coarsely chopped

1 clove garlic, smashed

1 bay leaf

1 head cauliflower, separated into florets

¼ teaspoon coriander seeds

1½ teaspoons salt

Rinse the cashews and soak in 3 cups of the water or stock at least 1 hour, or preferably overnight. Strain out the liquid and reserve. Set aside the cashews.

Heat the oil over medium heat in a large pot. Add the leeks, celery, garlic, and bay leaf and sauté the vegetables until translucent, 2 to 3 minutes. Add the cauliflower, coriander, salt, and the remaining 3 cups of water or stock along with the reserved cashew liquid. Bring to a boil, reduce to a simmer, cover, and cook until the cauliflower is soft, about 20 minutes. Discard the bay leaf. Place the contents in a blender with the soaked cashews and puree in batches until smooth.

"Cream" of Mushroom Soup

PREP TIME: 15 MINUTES   **COOK TIME:** 25 MINUTES
SERVES 2

Delicious cashew cream is also at work here, but this time with wild mushrooms, which have so much more flavor than the run-of-the-mill button variety.

2 tablespoons olive oil

1 pound mushrooms, trimmed and sliced
   (maitake, trumpet, enoki, shiitake, oyster)

1 cup chopped, well-washed leeks

3 cloves garlic, sliced

2 teaspoons fennel seeds

1 teaspoon coriander seeds

4 sprigs fresh thyme

1 bay leaf

⅓ cup raw cashews

2½ cups water or low-sodium vegetable stock

½ teaspoon salt

¼ teaspoon black pepper

In a large pot, heat the oil over medium-high heat. Add the mushrooms, leeks, garlic, fennel seeds, coriander seeds, thyme, and bay leaf and sauté until the mushrooms become soft, about 5 minutes. Add the cashews, water or stock, salt, and black pepper. Bring to a boil, reduce to a simmer, and cook for 15 minutes. Discard the thyme stems and bay leaf. Puree the soup in a blender, in batches if necessary, adjusting the consistency with more water or stock if desired.

Hearty Greens Soup with Farro

PREP TIME: 15 MINUTES   COOK TIME: 1 HOUR
SERVES 4

This is one of those recipes that I make early in the week and keep coming back to meal after meal. The farro continues to bloom as it soaks up the liquid flavored with the full-bodied vegetables, and with each bite, I feel like I'm getting all the goodness of grain and fiber and greens.

1 cup farro

8 cups water or low-sodium
vegetable stock

1 bunch collard greens

1 bunch Swiss chard

½ bunch kale

2 tablespoons olive oil

1 cup sliced, well-washed leeks

4 cloves garlic, sliced

3 sprigs fresh thyme

1 teaspoon coriander seeds

1 bay leaf

2 teaspoons salt

½ teaspoon black pepper

In a small pot, combine the farro with 3 cups of the water or stock. Bring to a boil, reduce to a simmer, and cook for 20 minutes.

Chop all the greens, stems included, into 1-inch pieces. In a large soup pot, heat the oil over medium-high heat. Add the leeks, garlic, thyme, coriander seeds, and bay leaf and sauté until the leeks are translucent, 5 to 7 minutes. Add the greens, salt, and black pepper, and cook for 1 minute. Add the entire contents of the small pot with the farro, plus the remaining 5 cups of water or stock. Bring to a simmer and cook until the farro becomes tender. Discard the thyme stems and bay leaf before serving.

Mushroom Consommé

PREP TIME: 5 MINUTES   **COOK TIME:** 15 MINUTES
SERVES 4

Consommé is the ultimate French classic. It's typically a clear broth with concentrated meat flavor, but in this version it's mushrooms that give it an intense, earthy flavor. This soup is perfect for dinner parties or the holidays—a little bowl afloat with whole wild mushrooms is an elegant, light way to start a meal and pique the taste buds' curiosity.

Note: If you're juice cleansing and using this recipe as your detox broth, consider using Bragg Liquid Aminos instead of soy sauce.

1 tablespoon olive oil

4 cloves garlic, sliced

1 cup sliced, well-washed leeks

¾ pound fresh mushrooms or 1 ounce dried

4 sprigs fresh thyme

8 cups water or low-sodium vegetable stock

2 tablespoons soy sauce or Bragg Liquid Aminos

½ teaspoon black pepper

Heat the oil in a large pot over medium heat. Add the garlic, leeks, mushrooms (if using fresh), and thyme and gently sauté until the vegetables are tender and translucent, 5 to 7 minutes. Be careful not to let them start to brown. Add the water or stock, mushrooms (if using dried), soy sauce or liquid aminos, and black pepper. Bring to a gentle simmer and cook for 10 minutes, or until the dried mushrooms rehydrate and flavor the soup. Discard the thyme stems.

Butternut Squash Soup Two Ways

I make butternut squash soup on a weekly basis during the fall and winter. It's pretty much the perfect recipe to have in your arsenal. The squash has its own natural creaminess, and its rich, sweet flavor gets even more complex with additional ingredients and garnishes. Try the Scarborough Fair Squash Soup (page 125) for a version that's earthy with fresh herbs, or the Marrakesh-Blend Squash Soup (page 126), which is perfumed with Middle Eastern spices. Throw in a simple garnish, like a drizzle of good balsamic vinegar, add a few cubes of Granny Smith apple or a handful of Spiced Pumpkin Seeds (page 127), and dinner becomes *dinner*.

CHEF'S TIP: GETTING INSIDE THAT SQUASH

When trying to open thick-skinned winter squashes, like acorn, kabocha, spaghetti, and butternut, the first trick is to not go for the machete chop. Push the tip of your knife an inch or two into the squash and work your way around the centerline. Once you've made the first pass, use the middle of your knife to cut through the softer flesh inside. For butternut squash in particular, cut at the base of the "neck," where it meets the round bottom. All the seeds are in the base, which you can halve and then clean out with a big spoon.

When I was starting out in the kitchen, I'd look for the smaller squashes until I got comfortable working them. It might be a procedure to get inside these guys, but it's worth the effort!

Scarborough Fair Squash Soup

PREP TIME: 15 MINUTES

COOK TIME: 45 MINUTES

SERVES 4

3 tablespoons olive oil

1 cup sliced, well-washed leeks

1 clove garlic, smashed

1 sprig fresh rosemary, 3 large fresh sage leaves, 2 sprigs fresh thyme,
    3 sprigs fresh parsley

1 bay leaf

1½-pound butternut squash, peeled, seeded, and cut into 1-inch cubes

1½ teaspoons salt

¼ teaspoon black pepper

6 cups water or low-sodium vegetable stock

In a large pot, heat the oil over medium heat. Add the leeks, garlic, bouquet garni, and bay leaf and sauté until the vegetables are tender but not starting to brown, 5 to 7 minutes. Add the squash, salt, and black pepper. Cook, stirring constantly, for 2 minutes. Add the water or stock, bring to a boil, then reduce to a simmer. Cook until the squash becomes very tender, 20 to 25 minutes. Remove the herb stems and bay leaf, puree the mixture in a blender—in batches if necessary—and serve.

Marrakesh-Blend Squash Soup

PREP TIME: 15 MINUTES   **COOK TIME:** 45 MINUTES

SERVES 4

3 tablespoons olive oil

1 cup sliced, well-washed leeks

1 clove, garlic, smashed

4 sprigs fresh thyme

1 bay leaf

1½ teaspoons ground cumin

½ teaspoon ground cinnamon

Pinch of cayenne pepper

1½-pound butternut squash, peeled, seeded, and cut into 1-inch cubes

1½ teaspoons salt

¼ teaspoon black pepper

6 cups water or low-sodium vegetable stock

Juice of ½ Meyer lemon (optional)

In a large pot, heat the oil over medium heat. Add the leeks, garlic, thyme, bay leaf, and spices and sauté until the leeks are tender but haven't begun to brown. Add the squash, salt, and black pepper and cook, stirring constantly, for 2 minutes. Add the water or stock, bring to a boil, then reduce to a simmer. Cook until the squash becomes very tender, 20 to 25 minutes. Remove the thyme stems and bay leaf, puree in a blender—in batches if necessary—add lemon juice to taste, if desired, and serve.

Spiced Pumpkin Seeds

TOTAL TIME: 5 MINUTES

In addition to being a lovely garnish for soups on the sweeter side, these are also perfect for a spicy, crunchy snack.

1 cup raw pumpkin seeds (sunflower seeds can be substituted)

1 tablespoon fresh lime juice

½ teaspoon pimenton or Spanish paprika

Pinch of cayenne pepper

½ teaspoon ground cumin

1 teaspoon sugar

¼ teaspoon salt

Combine all the ingredients in a medium-size sauté pan. Heat over low heat until fragrant and lightly brown, about 4 minutes. Stir frequently to avoid burning. Store in an airtight container.

Tomatillo Tortilla Soup

PREP TIME: 20 MINUTES
COOK TIME: 45 MINUTES
SERVES 4

Vegetable soup has gotten such a bad rap, but eating this dish is like having a little party. The yucca lends an exotic potatolike flavor that's sweeter and not as heavy as a white potato, the tomatillos add tangy zip, and the smoky red peppers make the soup that much sexier. When you top the whole thing off with Fritos-style crispy tortillas, you'll be wondering where the margaritas are. Have your kids help out with all the vegetable chopping, and the entire family can enjoy the festivity.

2 tablespoons olive oil

1 cup sliced, well-washed leeks

2 tablespoons finely chopped garlic

2 cups sliced tomatillos

½ teaspoon dried oregano

¼ teaspoon red pepper flakes

1 bay leaf

1½ teaspoons salt

¼ teaspoon black pepper

8 cups water or low-sodium vegetable stock

2 cups finely chopped yucca

1 recipe Homemade Fire-Roasted Peppers (recipe follows)

1 cup finely chopped zucchini

4 small corn tortillas, cut into 1-inch strips

½ cup parsley, coarsely chopped

1 tablespoon fresh oregano leaves, stripped from stem

In a large pot, heat the oil over medium-high heat. Add the leeks, garlic, and tomatillos and sauté until soft, about 3 minutes. Add the dried oregano, red pepper flakes, bay leaf, salt, black pepper, and water or stock and bring to a boil. Reduce to a simmer and add the yucca, cooking until it becomes soft and translucent, about 20 minutes. Add the roasted peppers and zucchini and cook for 10 minutes more. Discard the bay leaf.

Heat a large dry skillet over medium-high heat. Add the tortilla strips and pan-roast until crisp and brown, 5 to 7 minutes. Stir frequently to avoid burning.

Just before serving, sprinkle the soup with the tortilla strips, parsley, and fresh oregano.

Homemade Fire-Roasted Peppers

PREP TIME: 5 MINUTES **COOK TIME:** 20 MINUTES

This is a faster alternative to my Marinated Roasted Bell Peppers (page 160), and because you're using the flame of your burner or broiler instead of the heat of your oven, you'll get a more intense, smoky flavor. A poblano is a mild chili pepper with a little more heat than a bell pepper. I like using poblanos in Mexican-inspired dishes, but you can omit or substitute them as desired.

1 red bell pepper
1 yellow bell pepper
1 poblano pepper

Using a pair of tongs, char each pepper over an open flame (or under your broiler) until the skin is blackened and blistered on all sides. Place the peppers in a bowl and cover for 10 minutes to steam. Wash the peppers under running water to remove the outer charred layer and seeds. Slice into 1/4-inch pieces. Store in a covered container in the refrigerator.

Insert your paring knife about a half inch into the top of the tomato where the stem meets the flesh. Run the tip of your knife around the tough core until it's loose enough to pull out.

Better-Than-You've-Ever-Had Gazpacho

PREP TIME: 15 MINUTES

SERVES 6

Before Chris introduced me to this recipe, I thought I hated gazpacho. I liked the idea of a chilled soup bursting with fresh Spanish flavor, but in reality it always tasted like watered-down tomatoes with chunks of cucumber floating in it. The key, he taught me, is to use the best ingredients you can find. Because the recipe is so simple, things like high-quality olive oil and the freshest possible vegetables make a huge difference. Wait until the summertime when all you see at the farmers market are piles of gorgeous tomatoes that are still warm and perfumed from the sun. Instead of going for the typical red varieties, try using heirloom tomatoes, which come in a rainbow of colors and have a fruitier, less acidic taste.

VARIATION: For a creamy variation called *salmorejo*, add ½ cup of coarsely torn good-quality bread, like ciabatta or baguette, to the marinade.

4 large ripe heirloom tomatoes, cored and quartered

½ white onion, coarsely chopped

1 cucumber, coarsely chopped

2 cloves garlic, smashed

¼ cup olive oil

2 tablespoons white wine vinegar

½ teaspoon salt

½ teaspoon black pepper

¼ teaspoon red pepper flakes

In a medium-size bowl, combine all the ingredients, mix well, and chill for 1 hour to allow the vegetables to marinate. Puree in a blender until smooth, adjust the seasoning to taste, and serve cold.

Chilled Cucumber-Mint Soup

PREP TIME: 15 MINUTES
SERVES 3

Refreshing cucumbers and mint made creamy with pine nuts is the ultimate summer soup. Be sure to serve this the day you make it; otherwise the mint can oxidize and turn brown.

3 cucumbers, coarsely chopped
½ cup pine nuts
2 tablespoons olive oil
½ teaspoon salt
¼ teaspoon black pepper
½ cup fresh mint leaves

Place the cucumbers, pine nuts, oil, salt, and black pepper in a blender. Puree until smooth, about 2 minutes. Add the mint and puree until it is chopped, about 30 seconds. Chill before serving.

Citrus Salad with Roasted Fennel and Pomegranate

PREP TIME: 10 MINUTES   **COOK TIME:** 20 MINUTES   ·   SERVES 4

Once I was running out the door to catch a flight and realized I hadn't packed anything to eat (because I wouldn't be caught dead eating the slop the airlines pass off as food). I had this salad in my fridge, threw it in my bag, and was the envy of everyone on the plane when I unpacked it. It's such a simple way to enjoy citrus when it's at its peak, and the blend of these unique flavors makes for an impressively complex dish. You can use any variety of citrus, as long as it is in season. Serve it as a light lunch or an unexpected but lovely breakfast.

ROASTED FENNEL

1 fennel bulb, trimmed and quartered

1 teaspoon fresh lemon juice

6 tablespoons water or low-sodium
　　vegetable stock

½ teaspoon olive oil

¼ teaspoon salt

CITRUS SALAD

1 blood orange

1 Cara Cara orange

1 navel orange

1 Ruby Red grapefruit

¼ teaspoon salt

¼ teaspoon black pepper

Seeds from 1 pomegranate

2 tablespoons olive oil

Preheat oven to 350°F. Place all the fennel ingredients in a shallow baking dish small enough that the liquid comes about halfway up the fennel. Cover with foil and bake until the fennel is knife-tender, about 20 minutes. Remove and let cool completely.

To peel the citrus, first trim off the ends, creating a flat surface. Run your knife along the curvature of the fruit, removing all the rind and white pith. Cut into ¼-inch-thick rings and arrange them on a plate. If desired, cut the fennel into thinner slices. Scatter the fennel over the citrus. Season with the salt and black pepper, sprinkle with the pomegranate seeds, and drizzle with the olive oil. Serve at room temperature.

Warm Chayote Squash Salad
with Avocados and Arugula

PREP TIME: 20 MINUTES   **COOK TIME:** 25 MINUTES
SERVES 4

The first time I made this salad, I'd never even heard of chayote, so just finding it in the super-market was an experience. But it's a much more approachable squash than some of the others be-cause you don't have to bend over backward to get inside. Its flesh is mild and smooth and adds juicy sweetness to this warm winter salad.

2 chayote squashes, peeled and pits removed

1 tablespoon fresh lime juice

2 tablespoons olive oil

2 avocados, cut into large dice

¼ teaspoon salt

⅛ teaspoon black pepper

4 cups baby arugula

¼ cup Spiced Pumpkin Seeds (page 127)

Place the squashes in a small saucepot, cover with water, and simmer until fork-tender, about 25 minutes. Remove from the liquid and allow them to cool, then cut into 2-inch cubes.

In a small bowl, whisk together the lime juice and oil and set aside.

In a medium-size bowl, toss the avocados and the chayote with 2 tablespoons of the lime-juice mixture and half the salt and black pepper. Spread on a large plate or small platter.

In the same bowl, toss the arugula and pumpkin seeds with the remaining dressing and the remaining salt and black pepper. Pile on top of the avocados and squashes and serve.

Purple Potato Salad with Whole-Grain Mustard

PREP TIME: 10 MINUTES **COOK TIME:** 25 MINUTES
SERVES 4

This isn't your mother's potluck potato salad. Instead of smothering the potatoes in mayonnaise, you're showcasing the vegetables and all their potato goodness. This gorgeous purple variety is not only more festive-looking than its white-fleshed cousins, but because it's slow-digesting, you get more nutrients without spiking your blood sugar.

4 purple potatoes, cut into large dice
½ teaspoon salt
1 tablespoon whole-grain mustard
½ teaspoon olive oil
½ teaspoon sherry vinegar
½ cup diced celery
3 tablespoons coarsely chopped parsley
¼ teaspoon black pepper

In a large pot, place the potatoes and enough water to cover. Add the salt and bring to a boil. Reduce to a simmer and cook until fork-tender, about 15 minutes. Strain and place the potatoes in a medium-size mixing bowl. Add the mustard, oil, vinegar, celery, parsley, and black pepper. Gently toss to combine the ingredients, but not break apart the potatoes.

Boston Bibb Salad with Pistachios, Meyer Lemon, and Cucumber Ribbons

PREP TIME: 15 MINUTES

SERVES 4

Another great warm-weather dish. The thin cucumber ribbons soak up the dressing and look festive too!

½ English cucumber, peeled

1 head Bibb lettuce, washed and torn into bite-size pieces

¼ cup chopped fresh chives

¼ teaspoon salt

¼ teaspoon black pepper

¼ cup coarsely ground or chopped pistachios

2 tablespoons olive oil

Juice of ½ Meyer lemon

To make cucumber ribbons, gently run a vegetable peeler down the length of the cucumber. Stop when you get to the seeds and rotate to the next side until all that's left are seeds.

Place the lettuce, cucumber ribbons, and chives in a mixing bowl and season with the salt and black pepper. Add the pistachios, oil, and lemon juice and toss until the leaves are coated.

CHEF'S NOTE: MEYER LEMONS

This member of the citrus family may be more difficult to find, but the search is worth it. A hybrid of a lemon and an orange, Meyer lemons are more sweet than tart and lend a refreshing floral note to this vinaigrette. However, if you can't find them, feel free to use a regular lemon.

CHEF'S NOTE: "CHOPPING" HERBS

When handling fresh herbs, which can be delicate, be sure that your knife is sharp and that you're slicing rather than pounding. If not, the herbs can bruise and discolor.

Garbanzo Bean Dressing Two Ways

Garbanzo beans are a great base for dressing because they give it the body and texture you'd otherwise find in a caesar or creamy garlic dressing. The Garbanzo Bean Vinaigrette is perfect for light salads with more delicate lettuces, like Bibb, mesclun mix, arugula, and romaine, while the lemon-dill dressing can stand up to heartier salads made with lettuces like endive, radicchio, and chicory.

Garbanzo Bean Vinaigrette

PREP TIME: 10 MINUTES

MAKES ABOUT 2 CUPS

½ cup canned garbanzo beans, strained and rinsed, liquid reserved

¼ cup garbanzo-bean liquid (low-sodium vegetable stock or water may be substituted)

1 teaspoon Dijon mustard

¼ cup sherry vinegar

¾ cup olive oil

2 teaspoons maple syrup

¼ teaspoon salt

¼ teaspoon black pepper

In a blender, puree the garbanzo beans with the bean liquid, mustard, and vinegar until smooth. With the blender running, slowly pour in the oil to emulsify the dressing. Add the maple syrup and season with the salt and black pepper. Store in a lidded container in the refrigerator.

Garbanzo Bean Lemon-Dill Dressing

PREP TIME: 10 MINUTES
MAKES ABOUT 2 CUPS

1 cup canned garbanzo beans, strained and rinsed, liquid reserved

½ cup garbanzo-bean liquid (low-sodium vegetable stock or water may be substituted)

3 tablespoons fresh lemon juice

¼ cup olive oil

½ cup fresh parsley leaves

1 cup fresh dill fronds

1 teaspoon salt

¼ teaspoon black pepper

In a blender, puree the garbanzo beans, bean liquid, lemon juice, and oil until smooth. Add the parsley and dill and blend until the herbs are incorporated. Do not overmix, as the herbs will heat up and turn black. Season with the salt and black pepper. Store in a lidded container in the refrigerator.

Warm Haricot Verts Salad with Butter Beans, Hazelnuts, and Curry Vinaigrette

PREP TIME: 15 MINUTES   **COOK TIME:** 10 MINUTES · SERVES 4

Haricot verts are the American green bean's taller, thinner French cousin. Their flavor is almost exactly the same, as is the prep—blanched in boiling water for just a couple of minutes to keep them crisp and vibrantly green—so you can easily substitute one for the other. I love how the still-warm vegetables are complemented by the creamy, smoky beans and the sweet, crunchy hazelnuts.

CURRY VINAIGRETTE

1 (15.5-ounce) can butter beans, strained and rinsed, liquid reserved

3 tablespoons butter-bean liquid (low-sodium vegetable stock or water may be substituted)

¼ cup white vinegar

1 teaspoon curry powder

¾ cup olive oil

HARICOT VERTS SALAD

1 tablespoon salt, plus 1 teaspoon

12 ounces haricot verts, cut in half

½ cup hazelnuts, coarsely chopped

½ teaspoon black pepper

In a blender, puree ¼ cup of the beans with the bean liquid, vinegar, and curry powder until smooth. While the blender is still running, slowly add the oil to emulsify the dressing. Reserve.

Bring 2 quarts of water to a boil and add 1 tablespoon of the salt. Blanch the haricot verts for 2 minutes, strain, and immediately place in a large bowl. Toss with the remaining beans, ¼ cup of the dressing, and the hazelnuts. Season with the remaining 1 teaspoon salt and the black pepper.

Green Bean and Nicoise Olive Salad

PREP TIME: 15 MINUTES **COOK TIME:** 25 MINUTES • SERVES 4

This salad is a meal unto itself. The crisp green beans, meaty olives and potatoes, sweet, roasted tomatoes, and spicy arugula are just as exciting as they are filling.

1 tablespoon salt, plus 1 teaspoon

12 ounces green beans, trimmed

1 cup purple potatoes

1 tablespoon Dijon mustard

2 tablespoons red wine vinegar

6 tablespoons olive oil

1 cup Oven-Roasted Tomatoes (page 163)

½ cup nicoise olives, pitted

¼ cup sliced shallots

2 cups arugula

½ teaspoon black pepper

Bring a large pot of water to a boil and add 1 tablespoon of the salt. Blanch the beans for 2 minutes, then plunge immediately into ice water to stop the cooking. Drain and reserve.

In the same pot, place the potatoes and cover with cold water. Bring to a boil. Reduce to a simmer and cook until the potatoes are knife-tender. Drain, let cool completely, and halve or quarter them depending on their size.

In a large mixing bowl, whisk together the mustard and vinegar. While whisking constantly, slowly drizzle in the oil to emulsify the dressing. Add the green beans, potatoes, tomatoes, olives, shallots, arugula, remaining 1 teaspoon salt, and the black pepper. Toss to mix, and serve.

Chilled Soba Noodle Salad with Grilled Pineapple and Avocados

PREP TIME: 15 MINUTES   **COOK TIME:** 20 MINUTES

SERVES 4

All you need to serve with this lighter take on a pasta salad is a cold drink and some sunshine. Grilling the pineapple brings out all its succulent sweetness, which is perfectly matched by the bright Asian flavors of the dressing and fresh cilantro. Soba is a traditional Japanese noodle made from buckwheat, which is naturally gluten-free. Just make sure your brand doesn't mix in wheat flour, which does contain gluten.

This dish is great for making ahead, but hold off on mixing in the dressing until you're ready to serve.

Note: Soba cooks more quickly than pasta and is easy to boil into mushy oblivion. Test the noodles frequently; they should be served al dente.

1 tablespoon salt, plus
  ½ teaspoon
4 ounces dried soba
  noodles
2 teaspoons sesame oil
2 1-inch-thick slices
  pineapple
½ teaspoon black pepper
1 tablespoon olive oil, plus
  1 teaspoon

2 tablespoons sesame
  seeds
1 tablespoon minced fresh
  ginger
2 cloves garlic, minced
⅔ cup soy sauce or
  Bragg Liquid
  Aminos
2 tablespoons mirin
¼ cup water

2 tablespoons fresh lime juice

¼ teaspoon red pepper flakes

1½ ripe avocados, cut into
1-inch cubes

2 scallions, whites and greens,
chopped

¼ cup coarsely chopped fresh
cilantro

In a large pot, bring 2 quarts of water to a boil with 1 tablespoon of the salt. Add the soba noodles and cook until tender, 4 to 6 minutes. Drain and cool under cold water. Toss with 1 teaspoon of the sesame oil and reserve.

Season both sides of the pineapple slices with the remaining ½ teaspoon salt and the black pepper. Heat a grill, grill pan, griddle, or sauté pan over medium-high heat and add 1 tablespoon of the olive oil—or brush the grill pan, if using—or just enough so the pineapple won't stick. Add the pineapple to the grill or pan and cook so it caramelizes but doesn't burn, about 3 minutes per side. Remove and allow to cool completely. Cut into 1-inch cubes, making sure to discard the center core (it is lighter yellow than the flesh).

In a small dry pan, add the sesame seeds and toast over low heat until fragrant and lightly brown, about 5 minutes. Remove and let cool.

In the same pan, make the dressing. Heat the remaining 1 teaspoon olive oil over medium heat and cook the ginger and garlic until soft but not yet brown. Add the soy sauce or liquid aminos, mirin, and water and simmer for 1 minute. Remove from the heat and allow to cool completely. Add the remaining 1 teaspoon sesame oil, the lime juice, red pepper flakes, and sesame seeds.

In a large bowl, toss together the chilled soba noodles, pineapple, dressing, avocados, scallions, and cilantro. Serve chilled or at room temperature.

VEGGIES, VEGGIES, AND MORE VEGGIES

Unlike other cookbooks, the vegetable recipes here aren't relegated to side dishes and appetizers, or even lunch and dinner. That's because most of these recipes can step into any role—any meal of the day, any part of the meal. Mix and match a few or throw on a pot of whole grains and you've just made these dishes into a meal.

Don't Be a Potato Head

If you're scouring this section, looking for the familiar face of a white potato, you won't find it. Contrary to popular belief, they are not a staple. French fries and potato chips, despite what Congress has to say on the matter, are neither vegetables nor nutritious. In fact according to a Harvard School of Public Health study, starchy carbohydrates such as those found in white potatoes are to blame for things like obesity, diabetes, hypertension, and heart disease, and even nonfried versions were found to contribute to weight gain.

Roasted Root Vegetables

PREP TIME: 20 MINUTES   **COOK TIME:** 45 MINUTES
SERVES 4

Root vegetables like parsnips, carrots, sweet potatoes, turnips, and celery root are the bread and butter of the eat-from-the-ground world. Because they're so hearty, they're almost always available, and it's pretty darn hard to mess them up in the kitchen. I love roasting them because they get crispy and caramelized on the outside but creamy and sweet on the inside, with an intense concentration of their individual flavors. They're incredibly versatile, so feel free to mix and match veggie combinations with any variety of herbs and spices.

2 cups 1-inch pieces peeled parsnips

2 cups 1-inch pieces peeled carrots

2 cups 1-inch pieces peeled celery root

1 cup 1-inch-thick slices well-washed leeks

3 cloves garlic, unpeeled

2½ tablespoons olive oil

1 tablespoon chopped fresh rosemary

1 tablespoon chopped fresh thyme

1 teaspoon salt

½ teaspoon black pepper

¼ teaspoon fennel seeds

¼ teaspoon coriander seeds

1 bay leaf

¼ cup chopped fresh parsley

Preheat oven to 400°F.

Combine all the ingredients except the parsley in a large mixing bowl and toss until the vegetables are well seasoned. Spread the vegetables on a baking sheet and roast, stirring occasionally, until they are soft but not mushy, about 45 minutes. Remove from the oven, discard the bay leaf, and squeeze the garlic cloves from their skins. Sprinkle with the parsley and serve.

Braised Parsnips

PREP TIME: 10 MINUTES   **COOK TIME:** 20 MINUTES
SERVES 2

Braising is another great way to prepare root vegetables because your cooking liquid—which is rich with vegetable flavor once it reduces down—becomes a gravy.

2 tablespoons olive oil

4 parsnips, peeled and cut into ½-inch cubes

1 clove garlic, smashed

1 tablespoon chopped fresh thyme leaves

¼ teaspoon dried oregano

¼ teaspoon salt

⅛ teaspoon black pepper

1 cup low-sodium vegetable stock or water

2 tablespoons chopped fresh parsley

Over medium-high heat in a small sauté pan, heat the oil. Add the parsnips and garlic and cook until lightly browned, stirring twice, about 2 minutes. Season with the thyme, oregano, salt, and black pepper. Add the stock or water and simmer the parsnips until the liquid reduces to a thick syrup and the vegetables are soft and glazed, about 15 minutes. Remove from the heat, toss with the parsley, and serve.

CHEF'S NOTE:
THE HARDCORE
PARSNIP

Parsnips have a tough core running through them that can be a little too chewy even when cooked. To get around it, first cut the parsnips in half widthwise, so the thinner ends are separated from the thicker tops. Halve the thick tops lengthwise, exposing the core, which is lighter in color. Cut around it, discard, and slice the remaining parsnip as desired.

Orange and Ginger–Glazed Carrots

PREP TIME: 10 MINUTES   **COOK TIME:** 30 MINUTES
SERVES 2

This is another variation on braising where you're adding different aromatics to the cooking liquid. The sweetness of the orange and ginger really enhances the natural flavor of the carrots.

½ cup fresh carrot juice

½ cup fresh orange juice

¼-inch piece fresh ginger, peeled and cut into matchsticks

¼ teaspoon grated orange zest

¼ teaspoon salt

⅛ teaspoon black pepper

2 cups 1-inch pieces peeled carrots

Combine the juices, ginger, orange zest, salt, and black pepper in a small saucepot and bring to a simmer over medium heat. Add the carrots, stir once, turn the heat down slightly, then cover. Allow the mixture to simmer for 10 minutes, or until the carrots become tender. Remove the lid, increase the heat to medium-high, and continue to cook until the liquid reduces to a syrupy consistency, about 6 minutes. Remove from the heat and serve.

Whole Roasted Garlic

PREP TIME: 5 MINUTES   **COOK TIME:** 45 MINUTES TO 1 HOUR

MAKES 2 BULBS

Garlic is magical—there's hardly anything you can put it in that doesn't get better. And when you roast it whole, allowing it to get gooey in its own juices, it emerges a changed vegetable. In place of its intense, pungent flavor is a mellow sweetness that is delicious mixed into just about anything. Try adding it as a condiment to any of the dishes in this section, spreading it on good bread, swapping it in for raw garlic in dressings, tossing it with pasta, or even eating it on its own.

2 heads garlic

¼ teaspoon salt

Pinch of black pepper

1 tablespoon olive oil

1 sprig fresh thyme, cut in half

1 sprig fresh rosemary, cut in half

Preheat oven to 400°F.

Using a serrated knife, carefully cut through the top of each head of garlic three-quarters of the way through, exposing the cloves. Sprinkle the cloves with the salt, black pepper, and oil, then replace the "lids."

Create a small foil bundle for each head, enclosing the herbs. Roast for 45 minutes to 1 hour, or until the garlic is soft and the cloves easily slide from their husks.

Ginger-Miso Kale

PREP TIME: 5 MINUTES   **COOK TIME:** 10 MINUTES
SERVES 4

I can't tell you how many times I've gone to a restaurant and the only vegetable option is steamed and sad. Even in vegan restaurants you sometimes get a plate of soggy greens and some brown rice. It's like they can't figure out what to do with the vegetables either! Talk about giving veganism a bland reputation.

One trick I've learned is adding flavor to the cooking water. The miso and ginger bring out the amazing sweetness of the kale here, and because you're not steaming the vegetable within an inch of its life—no limp noodles!—it's good and it's good for you.

2 tablespoons miso paste

1 teaspoon minced fresh ginger

¾ teaspoon water

1 bunch each red and green kale, coarsely chopped or torn, tough stems
    trimmed (you can use just one or the other if necessary)

In a saucepot fitted with a lid, bring the miso, ginger, and water up to a simmer over medium heat. Add the kale, toss, and cover. Let steam for 2 minutes, remove the cover, and continue to cook until the greens wilt.

Roasted or Grilled Asparagus with Lemon

CHEF'S NOTE: THE POWER OF LEMON

When I can't put my finger on what a dish is missing—salt? pepper? heat?—I add a spritz of fresh lemon juice or a small tuft of zest. It's amazing how it can brighten a dish and bring it into perfect balance.

PREP TIME: 2 MINUTES   **COOK TIME:** 15 MINUTES
SERVES 4

Asparagus is one of the most abused vegetables out there. Too much heat and it gets brown and soggy, too little and it's bitter. But proper roasting or grilling enhances the vegetable's natural nuttiness, so all you need is a sprinkling of lemon juice and zest, a slick of olive oil, and a dash of salt and pepper for a minimalist but delicious dish.

1 bunch asparagus, tough bottoms snapped off
1 tablespoon olive oil
¼ teaspoon salt
¼ teaspoon black pepper
2 tablespoons fresh lemon juice
Zest of ½ lemon (small tuft)

Roasting: Preheat oven to 400°F.

In a mixing bowl, toss the asparagus with the oil, salt, and black pepper, then arrange on a baking sheet. Roast until fork-tender, about 15 minutes. Drizzle with the lemon juice, sprinkle with the lemon zest, and serve.

Grilling: Heat a grill over medium-high heat. After tossing the asparagus with the oil, salt, and black pepper, grill, turning frequently, until fork-tender, about 15 minutes. Finish as above.

Roasted Broccoli au Gratin

PREP TIME: 10 MINUTES   **COOK TIME:** 30 MINUTES
SERVES 4

This is my version of the American classic broccoli with cheese sauce. If you've been dousing your broccoli in Velveeta, it's probably because you're used to dealing with flavorless, limp broccoli. Roasting gives broccoli a deep, nutty flavor and crunchy texture that stands up on its own, but my Creamy "Cheese" Sauce (page 153) is an added bonus. Cauliflower and broccolini, a smaller, long-stemmed version of broccoli, also work well prepared this way.

1 head broccoli, cut into medium-size
 florets
½ teaspoon salt
¼ teaspoon black pepper
Pinch of red pepper flakes
2 tablespoons olive oil
Creamy "Cheese" Sauce (recipe follows)

Preheat oven to 400°F.

In a mixing bowl, toss the broccoli with the salt, black pepper, red pepper flakes, and oil. Arrange the florets on a baking sheet and roast until tender and a bit crispy, about 25 minutes. Spoon the cheese sauce over the roasted broccoli and bake for 3 minutes. Serve.

Creamy "Cheese" Sauce

PREP TIME: 5 MINUTES, PLUS OVERNIGHT

MAKES 2 CUPS

For when you just need a rich, gooey, oozy cheesy fix, this recipe will be your new best friend. I love this layered over vegetables for a quick au gratin, over pasta for mac 'n' cheese, or over Grilled Portabella Mushrooms (page 161) for a cheeseburger-inspired sandwich.

- 1 cup raw cashews, rinsed then soaked overnight with 1½ cups water
- 2 tablespoons nutritional yeast
- ¼ teaspoon salt

In a blender, puree the cashews and soaking liquid, nutritional yeast, and salt to create a smooth consistency. Add more water if necessary.

Brussels Sprouts Two Ways

If your family dinners were anything like mine growing up, then you're well acquainted with the soppy, soggy little cabbages known as Brussels sprouts. But these perfectly bite-size little guys are delicious *and* fun to eat if treated right. They can be sautéed and coated in a dressing like this creamy miso sauce or roasted to crunchy golden glory with fragrant, fresh rosemary.

Sautéed Brussels Sprouts with White Miso and Sesame Seeds

PREP TIME: 5 MINUTES   **COOK TIME:** 15 MINUTES
SERVES 4

2 tablespoons white miso paste

3 tablespoons warm water

1 tablespoon olive oil

1 pound Brussels sprouts, stems trimmed and cut in half

¼ teaspoon black pepper

3 tablespoons sesame seeds

In a medium-size mixing bowl, combine the miso paste and water and mix well. Set aside.

In a large sauté pan over medium-high heat, heat the oil, then cook the Brussels sprouts until they become fork-tender and caramelized, about 15 minutes. Add them to the bowl with the miso mixture, season with the black pepper, sprinkle with the sesame seeds, and serve.

Roasted Brussels Sprouts with Fresh Rosemary

PREP TIME: 5 MINUTES   **COOK TIME:** 25 MINUTES
SERVES 4

1 pound Brussels sprouts, stems trimmed
    and cut in half

2 tablespoons olive oil

½ teaspoon salt

¼ teaspoon black pepper

3 sprigs fresh rosemary

1 bay leaf

Preheat oven to 400°F.

In a medium-size mixing bowl, toss all the ingredients together, then arrange them evenly on a baking sheet. Roast 25 minutes, giving the tray a good shake halfway through, or until the Brussels sprouts are fork-tender and golden brown. Discard the bay leaf and rosemary stems.

Red Wine–Braised Cabbage

PREP TIME: 10 MINUTES **COOK TIME:** 1 HOUR
SERVES 6

This is a warm, robust dish that has a surprising sweet-and-sour flavor, like a mellow sauerkraut. The red cabbage gives it a gorgeous color, making it a very pretty addition to a potluck.

1 orange

½ cup fresh orange juice (about 1 orange)

1½ tablespoons olive oil

½ red onion, thinly sliced

1 clove garlic, thinly sliced

1 bay leaf

1 head red cabbage, cut in half lengthwise, cored, and cut into
    ¼-inch strips

1 cup red wine

1 tablespoon agave or maple syrup

1 teaspoon salt

¼ teaspoon black pepper

Using a vegetable peeler, remove the outer peel of the orange but none of the white pith. Reserve the peel. Juice the orange and add that juice to the ½ cup juice.

In a large heavy-bottomed pot, heat the oil over medium heat. Add the red onion, garlic, and bay leaf and cook until the onion softens but does not start to brown, about 3 minutes. Add the cabbage, wine, orange peel, orange juice, agave or maple syrup, and salt and black pepper. Cover and cook for 35 minutes, stirring occasionally. Remove the lid and continue cooking until the cabbage is tender and most of the liquid has reduced, about 25 minutes. Remove the orange peel and bay leaf and serve.

Broccoli Rabe with Garlic and Red Pepper Flakes

PREP TIME: 10 MINUTES   **COOK TIME:** 10 MINUTES   •   SERVES 2

I'm a huge red pepper flakes fan. You get just the right amount of punch and pick-me-up in anything you add them to. I love a simple sautéed vegetable with just garlic, but add some pepper flakes and woo! It's a party. They're great with a deep-green leafy vegetable like broccoli rabe, which is a kale-broccoli hybrid, and they enhance its nutty, bitter flavor. Just don't go too overboard with the flakes—a little pinch goes a long way.

1 bunch broccoli rabe

2 tablespoons olive oil

3 cloves garlic, sliced

¼ teaspoon red pepper flakes

½ teaspoon salt

¼ teaspoon black pepper

Chop the broccoli rabe into 2-inch pieces.

Over medium heat in a large sauté pan, heat 1 tablespoon of the oil. Add half the garlic and half the red pepper flakes and cook 1 minute, being careful not to let the garlic begin to brown. Add half the broccoli rabe and cook for 3 to 4 minutes, stirring frequently, until the stems become fork-tender but are still al dente. Remove from the pan and set aside. Repeat with the remaining oil, garlic, pepper flakes, and broccoli rabe.

Season the broccoli rabe with the salt and black pepper and serve.

Roasted Beets and White Balsamic Vinegar

PREP TIME: 15 MINUTES   **COOK TIME:** 1½ TO 2 HOURS
SERVES 4

Beets come in a range of beautiful colors, like golden yellow, rosy pink, and deep ruby red, and when roasted, they take on a wonderful earthy, meaty flavor. Don't be afraid just because they look dirty and kind of weird. Once they're cooked and soft, all you have to do is slip them out of their skins, drizzle them with oil and vinegar, and put them on the table. You can serve this dish warm or cold and play with different vinegars to bring out a range of flavors in the beets.

4 large beets, tops and roots removed and washed
½ teaspoon salt
¼ teaspoon black pepper
1 tablespoon chopped fresh herbs, such as chives, thyme, tarragon, or basil
1 tablespoon olive oil
1½ teaspoons white balsamic vinegar (may substitute cider, sherry, champagne, or white wine vinegar)

Preheat oven to 425°F.

Place the beets and 1 cup water in a shallow baking dish and cover with aluminum foil. Bake for 1½ to 2 hours, or until the beets become tender all the way through. A knife inserted in the center should slip easily in and out.

Remove the beets from the oven, uncover, and allow to cool enough so you can handle them. Wearing gloves or using a paper towel, gently wipe the beets to peel them.

Cut the beets into ¼-inch-thick slices and arrange on a plate. Sprinkle with the salt, black pepper, and herbs and drizzle with the oil and vinegar. Serve warm or chilled.

Marinated Roasted Bell Peppers

PREP TIME: 25 MINUTES, PLUS 2 HOURS TO MARINATE   **COOK TIME:** 25 MINUTES
SERVES 4

I like to keep a batch of these on hand because they're great for adding color and flavor and texture to just about anything, and they're perfectly happy sitting around in my fridge for a week or two. They're delicious on their own, as a side dish, or as antipasti, or you can throw them into some sautéed greens, toss them in a salad, or do what I love to do: make a roasted vegetable wrap with Grilled Portabella Mushrooms (page 161), asparagus, eggplant, and lettuce.

4 assorted bell peppers

2 cloves Whole Roasted Garlic (page 148)

½ teaspoon salt

¼ teaspoon black pepper

¼ teaspoon dried oregano

Pinch of red pepper flakes

1 small bay leaf

2 large sprigs fresh thyme

⅓ cup olive oil

3 tablespoons sherry vinegar

¼ cup pine nuts, toasted (optional)

Using a pair of tongs, char each pepper over an open flame or under the broiler until the skin is blackened and blistered on all sides. Place the peppers in a bowl and cover for 10 minutes to steam. When cool enough to handle, slit the bottom of each pepper with a knife and reserve any liquid. Wash the peppers under running water to remove the outer charred layer and the seeds. Slice the peppers into ¼-inch pieces and place in a small mixing bowl or shallow dish. Add the remaining ingredients, including the cooking liquid, cover, and refrigerate for at least 2 hours.

Grilled Portabella Mushrooms

PREP TIME: 5 MINUTES   **COOK TIME:** 20 MINUTES
SERVES 4

As far as I'm concerned, mushrooms are the meat of the vegan world. I like to grill them with some eggplant, then layer them all up on a bun with lettuce and tomato, or re-create a Philly cheesesteak with some of my Creamy "Cheese" Sauce (page 153). I brought these to a cookout just so I'd have something to eat while everyone else had their hamburgers and hot dogs, but once they caught a whiff of the delicious herb-and-garlic-scented mushrooms, they gobbled them up like sliders. I almost didn't get one myself! If you don't have an outdoor grill, these are just as delicious cooked up in a grill pan or sauté pan or on a griddle.

½ cup olive oil, plus 1 tablespoon if using a pan

⅓ cup balsamic vinegar

½ teaspoon salt

¼ teaspoon black pepper

4 sprigs fresh thyme

4 sprigs fresh rosemary

2 cloves garlic, thinly sliced

4 portabella mushroom caps

Combine the ½ cup oil, the vinegar, salt, black pepper, and herbs in a bowl. Insert the sliced garlic into the gills of the portabellas, being careful not to break the caps. Nestle the mushrooms in the marinade, making sure they're evenly coated. Heat a grill over a medium-high flame. Alternatively, heat a grill pan, sauté pan, or griddle over medium-high heat and add the remaining 1 tablespoon oil. Remove the mushroom caps from the marinade and lay them gill-side down, each with a sprig of rosemary and thyme underneath. Cook until the undersides are browned, about 5 minutes. Flip the caps over and cook 5 to 10 minutes more, until the mushrooms become tender. Remove any burnt garlic and herbs and serve.

Oven-Roasted Tomatoes

PREP TIME: 8 MINUTES   **COOK TIME:** 15 MINUTES
SERVES 2

Just when you thought a tomato is a tomato is a tomato, try one roasted. It's like eating the most decadent, sweet, rich tomato sauce you've ever had—and it's just a tomato! Because you're not stewing them down into mush, these tomatoes keep their shape while their skin beautifully puckers. Throw in some fresh herbs or chopped olives and you have a gorgeous side dish, a delicious afternoon snack, or the perfect garnish for a bowl of grains or "Spaghetti" with Fennel Seeds and Fresh Tomato Sauce (page 164).

1 pint cherry tomatoes

1 tablespoon olive oil

¼ teaspoon salt

Pinch of black pepper

1 tablespoon fresh thyme leaves

1 tablespoon chopped fresh basil (optional)

2 tablespoons chopped pitted nicoise olives (optional)

Preheat oven to 400°F.

Toss the tomatoes with the oil, salt, black pepper, and thyme and arrange on a baking sheet or in a sauté pan in which they fit in a single layer. Roast until the tomatoes just begin to blister, about 15 minutes. If desired, add the chopped basil or nicoise olives for the last 2 minutes of roasting. Continue cooking for another few minutes, until some of the tomatoes have begun to char and the skin puckers. Remove from the oven, place the tomatoes and any liquid they've released in a small bowl, and serve.

"Spaghetti" with Fennel Seeds and Fresh Tomato Sauce

PREP TIME: 10 MINUTES   COOK TIME: 30 TO 45 MINUTES
SERVES 4

Ever wonder what is inside some of those thick-skinned mystery squashes that you see in the dead of winter at the market? Well, spaghetti squash is aptly named because its flesh is made up of noodlelike strands that you can treat like pasta. When I first started making meals for myself, I'd boil up some already roasted spaghetti squash in plain water. It was so bland that I'd wonder what all the fuss was about. But adding the fennel seeds and bay leaf to the cooking water makes the squash really sing. It's delicious just like that or it can be dressed up for company with a dollop of Fresh Tomato Sauce (page 165) or Oven-Roasted Tomatoes (page 163).

1 medium-size spaghetti squash
   (1½ to 2 pounds)
½ teaspoon salt
¼ teaspoon black pepper
2 tablespoons olive oil

2 cups water
½ teaspoon fennel seeds
1 bay leaf
Fresh Tomato Sauce (recipe
   follows)

Preheat oven to 375°F.

Carefully cut the squash in half lengthwise and remove the seeds. Season the inside of both halves with the salt, black pepper, and oil. In a large roasting pan big enough to fit the squash, add the water, fennel seeds, and the bay leaf. Arrange the squash flesh-side down and cover the pan with foil. Roast 15 minutes, or until the undersides are caramelized, then flip the squash. Continue roasting until the squash is fork-tender, about another 15 minutes for a 1½-pound squash and 30 minutes for a 2-pound squash. Remove from the oven and allow the squash to cool.

Carefully scrape the "spaghetti" into a bowl and serve it with the Fresh Tomato Sauce.

Note: If desired, you can make a light sauce from the liquid in the roasting pan. Transfer the liquid to a small sauté pan, bring it to a fast simmer over medium-high heat, and allow it to reduce until thickened. Pour over the squash. You can serve the squash as is at this point or also add a dollop of tomato sauce.

Fresh Tomato Sauce

PREP TIME: 15 MINUTES   **COOK TIME:** 1 HOUR AND 15 MINUTES.
MAKES 8 CUPS

This classic sauce is a great one to have in your arsenal. Not only do you know exactly what's in it—instead of leaving it to chance with the jarred stuff—but you're using good, simple ingredients, so it tastes really fresh. Try it over rice, with spaghetti squash or pasta, or heaped on top of some roasted vegetables. Because the flavors only get better the longer they meld, keep a batch of this in your fridge for about a week or in the freezer and you'll have the foundation for a quick and easy dinner.

2 tablespoons olive oil

1 cup diced onion

3 cloves garlic, chopped

2 (28-oz) cans diced or crushed
    tomatoes

¼ cup red wine

1½ teaspoons dried basil

1 teaspoon dried oregano

¼ teaspoon red pepper flakes

1 bay leaf

½ teaspoon salt

¼ teaspoon black pepper

In a heavy-bottomed pot, heat the oil over medium heat. Add the onion and garlic and sauté until soft but not beginning to brown, about 3 minutes. Add the remaining ingredients and simmer for 1 hour, stirring occasionally to make sure the bottom of the sauce isn't burning. Discard the bay leaf before serving.

Swiss Chard with Coconut Curry

PREP TIME: 10 MINUTES   **COOK TIME:** 15 MINUTES
SERVES 2

This is the ultimate in steamed greens. Substituting coconut water for plain old tap water or stock, mixing in some spicy curry powder, and topping it all with crunchy coconut flakes takes this dish to a whole new level of exotic and delicious.

¼ cup grated unsweetened coconut

1 tablespoon coconut oil

1 teaspoon curry powder

½ cup coconut water

¼ teaspoon salt

1 bunch Swiss chard, leaves torn into large pieces, stems cut into ¼-inch pieces

Preheat oven to 350°F.

Spread the grated coconut on a baking sheet and toast until lightly golden brown, about 5 minutes. Remove and let cool.

Heat a large sauté pan or saucepot over medium-high heat. Add the coconut oil and curry powder and allow the curry to become aromatic, about 1 minute. Carefully add the coconut water and salt and bring up to a simmer. Add the chard leaves and stems, stir to combine all the ingredients, then cover. Let the mixture steam for 2 minutes. Remove the lid, stir, cover again, and continue to steam until the leaves are just wilted and tender and the stems are softened but still crunchy, about 5 minutes.

Remove from the heat, sprinkle with the toasted coconut, and serve.

Swiss Chard Italiano

PREP TIME: 5 MINUTES   **COOK TIME:** 15 MINUTES
SERVES 2

One of the greatest ways to develop your own repertoire in the kitchen is to play with flavors from cuisines you like. I love Italian food, which uses a lot of olive oil, garlic, and red pepper flakes to enhance whichever ingredient is the star. This simple combination works wonders with vegetables, and I particularly like it with leafy greens, such as Swiss chard.

- 1 tablespoon olive oil
- 2 cloves garlic, thinly sliced
- ¼ teaspoon red pepper flakes
- ½ cup low-sodium vegetable stock or water
- ¼ teaspoon salt
- ¼ teaspoon black pepper
- 1 bunch red or rainbow Swiss chard, leaves torn into large pieces, stems cut into ¼-inch pieces
- 3 tablespoons balsamic vinegar

Heat a large sauté pan over medium heat, then add the oil, garlic, and red pepper flakes. Sauté until the garlic softens but hasn't begun to brown. Carefully add the stock or water, season with the salt and black pepper, and bring to a simmer. Add the Swiss chard, stir to combine all the ingredients, then cover. Let the mixture steam for 2 minutes. Remove the lid, stir, cover again, and continue to steam until the leaves are just wilted and tender and the stems are softened but still crunchy, about 5 minutes.

Drizzle with the vinegar, give the leaves a quick toss, and serve.

Cauliflower Two Ways

Roasted cauliflower is surprisingly hearty in texture—meaty on the inside with a crisp, sweet, caramelized outside. The flavor is mild enough that it works well with all kinds of herbs and spices, and kids will love tossing all the ingredients together and watching the mixture change color. Let them get their hands dirty with these recipes and they'll be snacking on little veggie bites like popcorn.

Spicy Roasted Cauliflower with Pimenton

PREP TIME: 10 MINUTES   **COOK TIME:** 30 MINUTES   •   SERVES 4

Pimenton, or Spanish paprika, is a real party pleaser. It has a bright, spicy, smoky flavor and a vibrant red color that makes just about anything that much more delicious.

½ head cauliflower, cut into florets

1½ tablespoons olive oil

½ teaspoon salt

¼ teaspoon black pepper

¼ teaspoon coriander seeds

1 bay leaf

¼ teaspoon pimenton or Spanish paprika

¼ teaspoon chili powder

Preheat oven to 400°F.

In a large mixing bowl, toss the cauliflower, oil, salt, black pepper, coriander seeds, and bay leaf to coat.

Spread the cauliflower evenly on a baking sheet and roast in the oven, tossing every 10 minutes, for 30 minutes, or until it becomes tender and brown. Remove from the oven and let cool slightly. Discard the bay leaf.

Add the cauliflower back to the original mixing bowl and toss with the pimenton and chili powder until well coated.

Roasted Cauliflower with Tarragon and Lemon

PREP TIME: 5 MINUTES   **COOK TIME:** 30 MINUTES   •   SERVES 4

Normally when you think of roasting, the colder months come to mind. But the brightness of fresh tarragon and lemon zest takes this dish to a lighter, sunnier place.

½ head cauliflower, cut into florets
1½ tablespoons olive oil
½ teaspoon salt
¼ teaspoon black pepper
1 bay leaf

1 tablespoon chopped fresh
   tarragon leaves
Grated zest of ½ Meyer lemon
   (can also use regular lemon)

Preheat oven to 400°F.

In a large mixing bowl, toss the cauliflower, oil, salt, black pepper, and bay leaf to coat. Spread the cauliflower evenly on a baking sheet and roast in the oven, tossing every 10 minutes, for 30 minutes, or until it becomes tender and brown. Remove from the oven and let cool slightly. Discard the bay leaf.

Add the cauliflower back to the original mixing bowl and toss with the tarragon and lemon zest until well mixed.

Eggplant or Asparagus "Takeout" with Chinese Garlic Sauce

PREP TIME: 10 MINUTES   **COOK TIME:** 15 MINUTES   •   SERVES 4

This is my all-time favorite way to eat eggplant or asparagus. I tried this dish from every single Chinese restaurant in my neighborhood just to find the perfect version. Now that I make it without all that MSG and oil, I've finally found it! The vegetables are really the star here, but the sauce would fool anyone into thinking it's from your local take-out place.

EGGPLANT VARIATION

2 medium-size Japanese eggplants, cut into 1-inch pieces

1 tablespoon olive oil

2 teaspoons sliced garlic

2 teaspoons minced fresh ginger

2 scallions, whites and greens, chopped, 1 tablespoon of greens reserved

1 tablespoon balsamic vinegar

3 tablespoons soy sauce or Bragg Liquid Aminos

1 tablespoon mirin

½ teaspoon chili garlic paste

2 teaspoons maple syrup

1 recipe Basic Brown Rice (page 193)

Fill a large pot with water and, over high heat, bring it to a boil. Add the eggplants and cook until tender but not soft, 7 to 10 minutes. They should be mostly cooked through at this point, but not completely. Strain out the eggplants and reserve the cooking liquid.

In a medium-size sauté pan, heat the oil over medium-high heat. Add the garlic, ginger, and scallions. Cook until aromatic and soft but not browned. Add the vinegar, soy sauce or liquid aminos, mirin, chili garlic paste, maple syrup, and 1 cup of the reserved eggplant cooking liquid. Bring to a simmer, add the eggplants, and continue cooking until the eggplants are soft but not mushy and the sauce has begun to reduce and thicken, 5 to 7 minutes. Sprinkle with the reserved scallion greens and serve over brown rice.

ASPARAGUS VARIATION

1 tablespoon olive oil, plus more if necessary

1 bunch asparagus, coarse bottoms snapped off, cut into 1- to 2-inch pieces

1 clove garlic, sliced

2 teaspoons minced fresh ginger

2 scallions, whites and greens, chopped, 1 tablespoon of greens reserved

1 tablespoon balsamic vinegar

3 tablespoons soy sauce or Bragg Liquid Aminos

1 tablespoon mirin

½ teaspoon chili garlic paste

2 teaspoons maple syrup

⅓ cup water or low-sodium vegetable stock

1 recipe Basic Brown Rice (page 193)

In a medium-size sauté pan, heat the 1 tablespoon oil over medium-high heat. Add the asparagus and sauté until just cooked through, about 10 minutes. Remove and set aside. Add the garlic, ginger, and scallions to the pan, adding more oil if necessary, and cook until aromatic and soft but not browned. Add the vinegar, soy sauce, mirin, chili garlic paste, maple syrup, and water or stock. Bring to a simmer and cook until thickened slightly, 5 to 7 minutes. Add the asparagus, cook just to heat through, 1 to 2 minutes, then sprinkle with the reserved scallion greens and serve over the brown rice.

Pickled Vegetables

PREP TIME: 35 MINUTES, PLUS 2 HOURS TO OVERNIGHT TO PICKLE

COOK TIME: 5 MINUTES

While I like vegetables, I won't necessarily munch on a raw piece of carrot or celery. But I love nibbling on these light, not so in-your-face pickles. Unlike with store-bought pickles, this brine isn't insanely salty, and all the spices give the flavor a boost. And because of these pickles' probiotic qualities—meaning live bacteria is at work—they're great for digestion. Serve them chilled or at room temperature to complement your meal, or just have them on hand as a snack. They will keep in the fridge for about a month. When they start to discolor, it's time for them to go.

SALT BRINE

4 cups water

1 tablespoon salt

VEGETABLES

½ head cauliflower, cut into medium-size florets

4 stalks celery, cut into large matchsticks

3 large carrots, peeled, trimmed, and cut into large matchsticks

1 cucumber, cut into large matchsticks

3 cloves garlic, sliced

PICKLING BRINE

1 cup rice vinegar

2 cups water

1 bay leaf

½ teaspoon black peppercorns

½ teaspoon coriander seeds

½ teaspoon fennel seeds

½ teaspoon mustard seeds

1 teaspoon maple syrup

Combine the ingredients for the salt brine in a large bowl. Submerge the vegetables and let soak for 20 minutes.

In a small saucepot, combine all the pickling brine ingredients and bring to a boil. Cook for 2 minutes, remove from the heat, and allow to cool completely.

Combine both brines and the vegetables in a storage container and allow the mixture to sit for at least 2 hours or preferably overnight before serving. Store in the refrigerator.

Mixed Veggie Grill with Tangy BBQ Sauce

PREP TIME: 10 MINUTES   **COOK TIME:** 6 TO 12 MINUTES
SERVES 6

Grilling is my favorite way to get the most flavor out of vegetables. It lends a smokiness that accentuates vegetables' naturally nutty taste and brings out their surprisingly meaty texture. I love adding grilled veggies to wraps; topping them with Fresh Tomato Sauce (page 165) or Oven-Roasted Tomatoes (page 163) for a take on veggie marinara; or the ultimate: smothering them in Tangy BBQ Sauce (page 175) hot off the grill. Hell, pile them on a bun like a pulled pork sandwich!

These vegetables are just a few suggestions to get you started. This method works wonders with bell peppers, asparagus, corn, even tomatoes!

2 small eggplants, cut into ¾-inch-thick slices

2 zucchini, cut into ½-inch-thick slices

2 quartered portabella mushroom caps

2 yellow summer squashes, cut into ½-inch-thick slices

2 onions, cut into ¾-inch-thick slices

¼ cup olive oil, plus 1 tablespoon if using a pan

1 teaspoon salt

½ teaspoon black pepper

1 recipe Tangy BBQ Sauce (recipe follows)

In a large bowl, toss all the vegetables with the ¼ cup olive oil and the salt and black pepper until well coated. Heat a grill on high or a grill pan or sauté pan over medium-high heat (using the remaining 1 tablespoon of oil). Cook the vegetables for 3 to 4 minutes per side, 5 to 6 minutes for the mushrooms. After they've been flipped, generously brush the tops with Tangy BBQ Sauce and serve.

Tangy BBQ Sauce

PREP TIME: 5 MINUTES **COOK TIME:** 30 MINUTES
MAKES 2½ CUPS

Keep a batch of this in the fridge (it'll be good for about a month) or in the freezer during the summer and pull it out anytime the mood for barbeque strikes!

2 tablespoons olive oil
1 onion, coarsely chopped
2 cloves garlic, smashed
Pinch of red pepper flakes
1 teaspoon chili powder
1 teaspoon mustard seeds
⅓ cup apple cider
2 cups organic low-sugar ketchup
1 tablespoon maple syrup
½ teaspoon molasses

In a medium-size saucepot, heat the oil over medium heat. Add the onion and garlic and sauté until soft. Add the remaining ingredients and simmer for 20 to 30 minutes, thinning out with water if necessary. Remove from the heat and let cool. If desired, puree.

Zucchini and Summer Squash "Pasta"

PREP TIME: 20 MINUTES
SERVES 4

Using lemon to "cook" the vegetables is a traditional Italian technique, and it infuses this dish with bright, fresh flavor.

  2 zucchini

  2 yellow summer squashes

  2 tablespoons fresh lemon juice

  ¼ cup chopped fresh chives

  ¼ teaspoon salt

  ¼ teaspoon black pepper

  1 tablespoon fresh oregano leaves

For the "pasta," gently run a vegetable peeler down the length of the zucchini and yellow squashes to make thin ribbons. Stop when you get to the seeds and rotate to the next side until all that's left are seeds. Toss the ribbons with the rest of the ingredients, let sit for at least 10 minutes so the flavors can incorporate, and serve.

Whole Roasted Eggplant

PREP TIME: 5 MINUTES   COOK TIME: 45 MINUTES
SERVES 4

Roasted eggplant is the ultimate blank canvas. The rich, custardy flesh becomes the perfect base for all manner of herbs, spices, and toppings. Heap it with Moroccan-Spiced Apricot Topping (page 180) and Egyptian Dukkah (page 181) for an impressive meal, or mix just the flesh with a minced clove of garlic, a drizzle of olive oil, and a handful of fresh parsley to make a deceivingly sophisticated spread. Add a loaf of good bread or a bowlful of hearty grains, and you have a meal!

5 tablespoons olive oil

1 large eggplant, cut in half lengthwise

½ teaspoon salt

¼ teaspoon black pepper

1 teaspoon dried basil

Preheat oven to 400°F.

Grease a baking sheet with 1 tablespoon of the oil. Lay the eggplant on the sheet flesh-side up. With the tip of your knife, make crosshatches on each half of the eggplant, cutting into the flesh but not deep enough to cut through the skin. Drizzle with the remaining 4 tablespoons oil and season with the salt, black pepper, and basil, making sure to rub the mixture into the crosshatching. Flip the eggplant over so it's now flesh-side down. Roast in the oven for 15 minutes, then carefully flip the eggplant over and continue roasting for another 30 minutes, or until the flesh is tender but not too soft. The eggplant should keep its shape but open up along the crosshatching. Remove and allow to cool slightly before serving.

Moroccan-Spiced Apricot Topping

PREP TIME: 10 MINUTES   **COOK TIME:** 15 MINUTES
MAKES 2 CUPS

This heady mix of spices and apricots makes almost anything more decadent. Try it spooned over roasted eggplant as a main course or mounded on some good bread as an appetizer.

1 tablespoon olive oil

1 onion, diced

1½ teaspoons minced fresh ginger

½ teaspoon salt

¼ teaspoon black pepper

1 teaspoon ground cinnamon

1 teaspoon ground cumin

½ teaspoon ground coriander

Pinch of cayenne

3 tablespoons water or low-sodium vegetable stock

½ cup chopped apricots, dried or fresh

3 tablespoons chopped fresh parsley

Juice of ½ lemon

Heat the oil in a sauté pan over medium-high heat. Add the onion and ginger and sauté 3 minutes. Stir in the salt and black pepper and the spices and allow to toast 1 minute. Pour in the water or stock, reduce the heat to medium, and cover. Cook until the onion is soft, about 8 minutes. Stir in the apricots and parsley. Remove from the heat, drizzle with the lemon juice, and serve.

Egyptian Dukkah

PREP TIME: 15 MINUTES

MAKES ABOUT 2 CUPS

In Egypt they dip their bread into olive oil, then into a bowl of dukkah, a rich, spicy distant cousin of bread crumbs. I use dukkah as another seasoning in my collection and sprinkle it onto vegetable dishes for a little extra something. It's also great as a bread crumb–like topping over Roasted Broccoli au Gratin (page 152) and "Spaghetti" with Fennel Seeds and Fresh Tomato Sauce (page 164).

⅔ cup hazelnuts

½ cup sesame seeds

2 tablespoons coriander seeds

2 tablespoons cumin seeds

1 teaspoon salt

½ teaspoon black pepper

Preheat oven to 350°F.

Spread the hazelnuts on a baking sheet and toast in the oven for 4 minutes. Remove and let cool.

In a small dry skillet over medium heat, toast the sesame seeds until fragrant and golden brown, about 3 minutes. Remove and let cool.

Next toast the coriander seeds and cumin seeds until fragrant, about 3 minutes. Working in batches, pulse in a spice grinder until finely ground. Repeat with the hazelnuts, stopping at a coarser texture if desired. In a medium-size bowl, combine the nuts, sesame seeds, and ground coriander and cumin. Mix in the salt and black pepper.

Ratatouille

PREP TIME: 25 MINUTES

COOK TIME: 1 HOUR AND 15 MINUTES

SERVES 4

This dish is traditionally French and is just as rustic and beautiful as it is hearty and delicious. The layers of vegetables melt into one another, and their colorful arrangement makes for an impressive presentation.

⅓ cup olive oil

3 onions, sliced

1 teaspoon salt

½ cup fresh thyme leaves

2 teaspoons sherry vinegar

2 yellow summer squashes, sliced into ¼-inch-thick rounds

2 zucchini, sliced into ¼-inch-thick rounds

2 small eggplants, cut in half lengthwise, then sliced into
    ¼-inch-thick half-moons

4 tomatoes, cut in half, then sliced into ¼-inch-thick half-moons

1 teaspoon black pepper

Preheat oven to 375°F.

In a large pot, heat 2 tablespoons of the oil over medium heat. Add the onions and ½ teaspoon of the salt and cover. Turn the heat down slightly and sauté the onions until translucent and soft but not beginning to brown, about 20 minutes. Remove the lid, add 2 tablespoons of the thyme and the vinegar, and cook while stirring for 2 minutes. Transfer the onions to a shallow 9 x 13 baking dish or a baking sheet with sides. Spread them evenly so they can cool to room temperature.

Arrange the remaining vegetables on top of the onions, creating even, alternating layers of each. Season with the remaining ½ teaspoon salt, the black pepper, and the remaining 6 tablespoons thyme and drizzle with the remaining 3⅓ tablespoons oil. Cover with foil and bake in the oven for 45 minutes, or until the vegetables are tender. Be careful when checking under the foil, as steam will have built up and can burn you.

When the vegetables are done, take the baking dish out of the oven, carefully remove the foil, and return the dish to the oven for 5 minutes more. Remove from the oven, allow to cool, and serve.

Eggplant Caponata

PREP TIME: 10 MINUTES   **COOK TIME:** 15 MINUTES
SERVES 4 TO 6

Caponata is a real workhorse. The earthy, complex blend of sweet raisins, crunchy pine nuts, and meaty eggplant—made that much more rich and tomato-y by surprise-guest cocoa powder—is just as at home on a bed of grains as it is on its own as a side dish or layered on toasted bread.

2 tablespoons olive oil

1 cup diced onion

2 cloves garlic, sliced

½ cup tomato paste

1 teaspoon cocoa powder

Pinch of red pepper flakes

2 medium-size eggplants, cut into ½-inch cubes

¼ cup water

⅓ cup white wine vinegar

3 tablespoons golden raisins

3 tablespoons pine nuts

1 teaspoon salt

½ teaspoon black pepper

1 teaspoon dried oregano

1 tablespoon chopped fresh basil

In a large saucepot, heat the oil over medium heat. Add the onion and garlic and sauté until soft. Add the tomato paste, cocoa powder, and red pepper flakes and cook for 1 minute. Add the eggplants, water, vinegar, raisins, pine nuts, salt, black pepper, and oregano. Cover and cook until the eggplants soften, about 10 minutes. Sprinkle with the basil and serve.

Marinated Wild Mushrooms

PREP TIME: 10 MINUTES, PLUS 2 HOURS TO OVERNIGHT FOR MARINATING
COOK TIME: 5 MINUTES
SERVES 8

Inspired by Italian trattorias, I like to put out a spread of cold appetizers for guests to nibble on while I make dinner. These mushrooms do just the trick, and because I use all kinds of neat-looking wild varieties, it looks way more difficult to make than it actually is.

¼ teaspoon coriander seeds

¼ teaspoon fennel seeds

2 cloves garlic, smashed

½ teaspoon dried oregano

½ teaspoon grated lemon zest

¼ cup fresh lemon juice

¼ cup sherry vinegar

¼ cup olive oil

1 bay leaf

½ teaspoon salt

¼ teaspoon black pepper

2 tablespoons chopped fresh parsley

1 pound mixed wild mushrooms, such
    as shiitake, oyster, and maitake,
    chopped into 1-inch pieces

Crush the coriander and fennel seeds to break them open (pressing down on a cutting board with the back of a skillet works well). Transfer to a small saucepot.

Add the rest of the ingredients except the mushrooms to the pot and over medium heat bring to a simmer. Cook the marinade for 3 minutes. Remove from the heat and allow to cool slightly.

Place the mushrooms in a large mixing bowl and pour the marinade over them. Marinate the mushrooms at least 2 hours or preferably overnight in the refrigerator. Serve at room temperature.

Mashed Potatoes with Wild Mushroom Gravy

PREP TIME: 25 MINUTES   **COOK TIME:** 1 HOUR AND 15 MINUTES
SERVES 4 TO 6

If there is one recipe that can single-handedly prove that special-occasion food can still be delicious without meat, cream, or butter, this is it. The mashed potatoes—made with the purple variety that actually delivers nutrition, versus their white counterparts—are fluffy and creamy and light. And when you stew mushrooms in a bath of red wine and herbs, you get all the rich, hearty flavor you expect from gravy.

MASHED POTATOES

5 medium-size purple potatoes, peeled and quartered

¾ teaspoon salt

½ cup plus 2 tablespoons olive oil

¼ teaspoon black pepper

MUSHROOM GRAVY

2 tablespoons rice flour

¾ cup water

2 tablespoons olive oil

1 cup diced onion

3 cloves garlic, sliced

12 ounces mixed wild mushrooms, such as shiitake, oyster, and maitake,
    cut into ¼-inch pieces

1 teaspoon chopped fresh rosemary

1 teaspoon fresh thyme leaves

2 teaspoons chopped fresh sage

¼ teaspoon black pepper

1 tablespoon soy sauce or Bragg Liquid Aminos

½ cup red wine

1 tablespoon balsamic vinegar

Place the potatoes and ½ teaspoon of the salt in a large saucepot and add enough cold water to cover. Bring to a boil over high heat, reduce to a simmer, and cook until the potatoes yield to a knife. Drain and pass the potatoes through a ricer or food mill into a bowl. You can also mash by hand. Gradually add the oil, mixing to incorporate. Season with the remaining ¼ teaspoon salt and the black pepper.

Meanwhile make the gravy. In a small bowl, combine the rice flour with the water. Reserve.

In a large skillet, heat the oil over medium heat. Add the onion and garlic and sauté until the onion is translucent. Add the mushrooms, herbs, and black pepper and sauté until the mushrooms release their liquid, 5 to 7 minutes. Add the soy sauce or liquid aminos, wine, and vinegar and cook until the liquid reduces by half. Stir in the flour-water mixture and cook until the entire mixture is thickened.

Serve the mashed potatoes with the gravy.

Roasted Artichoke Hearts with Walnut-Arugula Pesto

PREP TIME: 10 MINUTES **COOK TIME:** 1 HOUR
SERVES 4

Serving whole artichokes is not only an unexpected and beautiful presentation but it's a fun project for everyone at the table. All hands will be occupied with tearing through the leaves, dunking them into pesto, and, bit by bit, making it closer to the delicious heart. It's like a little treasure hunt!

Juice of 1 lemon
4 large artichokes
Salt and black pepper to taste
Walnut-Arugula Pesto (recipe follows)

Preheat oven to 400°F.

In a large bowl, combine the lemon juice with about 6 cups of water, or enough to cover 3 artichokes. This will help keep the trimmed artichokes from turning brown as you work.

Using a serrated knife, trim 1 inch from the tops of the artichokes. Also trim the bases where the stems meet the artichokes. Place each artichoke in the lemon water as you've finished.

Pat the artichokes dry and season with a pinch of salt and black pepper. Arrange them on a baking sheet and roast in the oven until fork-tender, about 1 hour. Remove from the oven and allow to cool.

When cool enough to handle, serve with Walnut-Arugula Pesto.

To eat, pull away the tough outer leaves until you get to those that are more tender and light green. At the base of each leaf is a bit of "meat" that you can dip in the pesto and scrape off with your teeth. Continue peeling away the leaves until you get to the furry center of the artichoke, or the "heart." Use the side of a teaspoon to scrape away the fur and discard. Smother the heart in pesto and devour.

Walnut-Arugula Pesto

PREP TIME: 5 MINUTES
MAKES 1 CUP

Pesto purists might say this doesn't qualify because traditional recipes call for Parmesan, but to that I say, "Who cares?!" You can still make a nutty, creamy, herby spread that's unbelievably delicious slathered on just about anything.

    1 cup walnuts
    2 cups arugula
    ¼ cup packed fresh basil leaves
    2 cloves garlic, peeled
    3 tablespoons olive oil
    ⅛ teaspoon salt
    ⅛ teaspoon black pepper

Combine all the ingredients in a blender or food processor and pulse until smooth but still chunky.

Candied Sweet Potatoes with Apples

PREP TIME: 10 MINUTES   **COOK TIME:** 1 HOUR
SERVES 6

For my first Thanksgiving as a vegan, I celebrated with a group of girlfriends. Everyone was responsible for bringing something, and I brought a variation of this dish. It was so much fun going around the table and applauding each person's efforts—and in turn getting my own applause— and my vegan casserole was right at home with the other traditional holiday staples.

4 large sweet potatoes

2 Granny Smith apples

4 tablespoons vegetable spread, such as Earth Balance

½ cup maple syrup

2 teaspoons ground cinnamon

¼ teaspoon ground nutmeg

½ teaspoon salt

¼ teaspoon black pepper

Preheat oven to 400°F.

Wrap the sweet potatoes in aluminum foil and bake in the oven for 40 minutes or until just fork-tender. Remove from the oven and let cool until they can be handled. Cut into ½-inch-thick slices. Keep the oven on.

Peel and core the apples, then slice them into ½-inch-thick pieces.

Arrange the sweet potatoes in a 9 x 13 baking dish, alternating with the apples. Dot with the vegetable spread, drizzle with the maple syrup, and sprinkle with the cinnamon, nutmeg, salt, and black pepper. Bake for 15 minutes, or until the maple syrup starts to bubble.

Spring Pea Medley with Sweet Corn and Fire-Roasted Red Peppers

PREP TIME: 10 MINUTES   **COOK TIME:** 10 MINUTES
SERVES 4 TO 6

The first time I made this dish, it brought back memories of the bland frozen mixes my mom would make us eat. But then I realized that when you're cooking with peas and corn at the peak of their season, it's a whole different ball game. It just tastes so alive—sweet and full of fresh flavor.

1 cup water

1 clove garlic, sliced

2 cups sugar snap peas

2 cups English peas

2 cups sweet corn

3 scallions, whites and greens, sliced

1 cup Homemade Fire-Roasted Red Peppers (page 129), ¼-inch-thick slices

⅓ cup chopped fresh parsley

1 teaspoon grated lemon zest

½ teaspoon fresh lemon juice

½ teaspoon olive oil

½ teaspoon salt

¼ teaspoon black pepper

In a medium-size sauté pan over medium heat, bring the water to a simmer and add the garlic. Add the peas, corn, and scallions and cook until heated through, about 2 minutes. Add the peppers and let cook for another minute. Remove from the heat and add the parsley, lemon zest and juice, oil, and the salt and black pepper. Serve warm, chilled, or at room temperature.

GRAINS

THE BASICS

Simple whole grains go a long way toward making vegetable dishes into hearty main courses and are the perfect snack with just a little bit of dressing or olive oil. I make a big batch at the beginning of the week so all I have to do at mealtime is grab some out of the fridge. Here are basic recipes for the two grains that are my go-tos: brown rice and quinoa. They're incredibly versatile, nutrient-dense, and, best of all, delicious!

Basic Brown Rice

COOK TIME: 35 MINUTES

MAKES 3 CUPS

Brown rice is just one example in the wonderful world of variation in rice. Yellow, wild, basmati, short-grain, long-grain—they're all so beautiful and aromatic. It makes me wonder how people get stuck with Uncle Ben's! You can apply this same 3:1 ratio to almost all of the different types of this grain.

- 1 cup brown rice
- 3 cups water
- ¼ teaspoon salt

Rinse the rice under running water to wash off the excess starch. Place in a medium sauce-pot with the water and salt. Bring up to a boil, reduce to a simmer, then cover and cook 35 minutes, or until tender. Do Not Uncover or Stir. Turn off the flame and allow the rice to steam with the lid on for another 5 minutes. Fluff with a fork and serve, or let cool and store in the fridge for a week.

Basic Quinoa

COOK TIME: 15 MINUTES
MAKES 3 CUPS

1 cup quinoa

2 cups water

¼ teaspoon salt

1 bay leaf

In a small saucepot bring all the ingredients up to a boil, reduce to a simmer, then cover. Cook until the quinoa is tender and the water is absorbed, about 15 minutes. Discard the bay leaf. Serve warm or spread out on a baking sheet to cool quickly for cold salads or storage.

Basic Polenta

PREP TIME: 10 MINUTES   COOK TIME: 50 MINUTES
SERVES 6

Polenta, or ground cornmeal, is like Italian grits. You can serve it creamy and fresh out of the pot, or let it set, and grill, sauté, or bake it. The outside will get crisp and brown while the inside stays soft and smooth.

- 1 tablespoon olive oil, plus 1½ teaspoons olive oil for greasing the pan
- 3 cups almond milk
- 1 clove garlic, minced
- 1½ cups finely chopped, well-washed leeks, whites and greens
- ½ teaspoon salt
- ¼ teaspoon black pepper
- ¾ cup yellow cornmeal

Lightly grease a small baking pan with 1½ teaspoons of the oil. In a medium-size saucepot, bring the almond milk, garlic, leeks, remaining 1 tablespoon oil, and the salt and black pepper to a simmer. Slowly whisk in the cornmeal. Continue stirring with a wooden spoon until the polenta has thickened. Serve at this point if desired, or transfer to the prepared pan and allow to set completely, 30 to 40 minutes. Flip the polenta out of the pan and onto a cutting board. Slice into squares. Grill or pan-sear over medium heat, about 5 minutes on each side, or bake at 400ºF degrees for 10 minutes, flipping after 5 minutes. The polenta squares should be golden brown and heated throughout.

Wild Mushroom Risotto

PREP TIME: 15 MINUTES

COOK TIME: 45 MINUTES

SERVES 6

I don't know anyone who doesn't love risotto. It's creamy, it's rich, and it's completely decadent. But with all that cheese and oil and butter, you can never have more than a couple of bites. This version, however, is every bit as indulgent, but you can clean your bowl and feel good about it.

Note: This recipe uses Arborio rice, which is the grain traditionally used in the Italian dish and is essentially white rice. You can easily substitute farro, which is another Italian grain that's much higher in protein, fiber, and nutrients and has a delicious nutty taste.

WILD MUSHROOM MIXTURE

2 tablespoons olive oil

½ cup finely diced onion

1 clove garlic, sliced

1 cup sliced shiitake mushrooms

1 cup sliced oyster mushrooms

1 cup sliced maitake mushrooms

1 tablespoon fresh thyme leaves

¼ teaspoon salt

¼ teaspoon black pepper

RISOTTO

2 tablespoons olive oil

½ cup finely diced onion

1 clove garlic, sliced

1 tablespoon fresh thyme leaves

1½ cups Arborio rice

½ cup white wine

5 cups water or low-sodium
vegetable stock

3 tablespoons nutritional yeast

2 teaspoons salt

½ teaspoon black pepper

In a large pot or sauté pan, heat the oil for the mushroom mixture over medium heat. Add the onion, garlic, mushrooms, and thyme and sauté to soften, 5 to 8 minutes. Season with the salt and black pepper, transfer to a bowl, and reserve.

To the same pot, over medium heat, add the oil for the risotto. Add the onion, garlic, and thyme and cook until soft, about 3 minutes. Add the rice and toast for 2 minutes. Pour in the wine and cook 1 minute, scraping any browned bits off the bottom of the pot.

Add 2 cups of the water or stock and turn the heat to high. Bring to a boil, then lower the heat back to medium. Allow the risotto to simmer, stirring every 2 minutes, until the liquid reduces down by half. Add 2 more cups of water or stock and repeat. Add the remaining 1 cup of water or stock and stir frequently until most of the liquid has been absorbed by the rice but the rice is still loose. Add the wild mushroom mixture back to the pot, stir in the nutritional yeast, and season with the salt and black pepper. Serve immediately.

Couscous Two Ways

Although couscous isn't technically a whole grain—it's made from a wheat or semolina-based dough and formed into tiny pellets (or larger ones in the case of Israeli couscous)—it's so easy to make and pairs with such a variety of vegetables and herbs, I recommend adding it to your recipe stash. You can serve it as a cold salad, with refreshing garnishes like cucumber and mint, or hot with hearty, fragrant adornments like sundried tomatoes and Kalamata olives.

Chilled Couscous with Cucumber and Mint

PREP TIME: 10 MINUTES, PLUS 30 MINUTES TO CHILL

COOK TIME: 10 MINUTES

SERVES 6

1 cup couscous

2 cups low-sodium vegetable stock or water

1 cup diced cucumber

½ cup chopped scallions, whites and greens

¼ cup fresh mint leaves, coarsely chopped

¼ cup *pepitas*, pine nuts, or sliced almonds,
    raw and unsalted

2 tablespoons fresh lemon juice

1 tablespoon olive oil

½ teaspoon salt

¼ teaspoon black pepper

Place the couscous in a small heatproof mixing bowl.

In a small saucepot over high heat, bring the vegetable stock or water to a boil. Immediately pour the liquid over the couscous, cover, and let steam for 8 minutes. Fluff with a fork and let chill in the refrigerator. For quicker chilling, spread the couscous out on a baking sheet.

Once the couscous has chilled completely, combine it with the rest of the ingredients.

Israeli Couscous with Sundried Tomatoes and Kalamata Olives

PREP TIME: 10 MINUTES   **COOK TIME:** 25 MINUTES
SERVES 6

1 tablespoon olive oil

½ cup sliced, well-washed leeks, whites and greens

1 clove garlic, sliced

1 cup Israeli couscous

3 cups low-sodium vegetable stock or water

½ cup chopped sundried tomatoes

¼ cup pitted and chopped Kalamata olives

1 tablespoon fresh oregano leaves

¼ cup chopped fresh basil

½ teaspoon salt

¼ teaspoon black pepper

In a medium-size saucepot, heat the oil over medium heat and add the leeks and garlic. Cook until softened, about 2 minutes, then add the couscous and toast slightly, 2 more minutes. Add the stock or water and bring to a simmer. When the liquid is almost all absorbed, add the sundried tomatoes. Remove from the heat and mix in the olives, herbs, and the salt and black pepper.

Corn Bread Stuffing

PREP TIME: 20 MINUTES   **COOK TIME:** 45 MINUTES TO 1 HOUR
SERVES 6 TO 8

For me, ever since I was little, Thanksgiving was all about the sides—I couldn't have cared less about the turkey! When you have a table brimming with irresistible, feast-worthy dishes like this stuffing, who wants to save room for that drumstick?

The corn bread is also delicious dressed up with red bell pepper, scallions, or jalapeños and served on its own. If you're making it for the stuffing, however, it's a good idea to make it the day before and let it dry out slightly so it absorbs all the stuffing juices.

CORN BREAD
1 teaspoon olive oil
1 cup yellow cornmeal
1 cup rice flour
1 tablespoon baking powder
½ teaspoon salt
2 tablespoons egg replacer mixed with 6 tablespoons water
1 cup almond milk
3 tablespoons vegetable spread, such as Earth Balance, melted
2 tablespoons maple syrup
⅓ cup corn
⅓ cup chopped red bell pepper, scallions, or jalapeños, (optional)

Preheat oven to 400°F.

Lightly oil a 9-inch round cake pan with the 1 teaspoon oil. In a large mixing bowl, combine the dry ingredients. In a separate small bowl, combine the wet ingredients, including the egg replacer–water mixture. Add the wet ingredients to the dry ingredients and mix until evenly incorporated. Stir in the corn and the bell pepper, scallions, or jalapeños, if using, and pour into the prepared pan. Bake until golden brown and a knife comes out clean when inserted in the center, 25 to 30 minutes. Remove from the oven and let cool on a wire rack.

STUFFING

2 tablespoons olive oil

1½ cups sliced, well-washed leeks, whites and greens

½ cup diced celery

1 clove garlic, sliced

4 cups crumbled 1-day-old corn bread

1 bay leaf

1 tablespoon fresh thyme leaves

1 tablespoon chopped fresh sage

½ cup coarsely chopped pecans

2 cups low-sodium vegetable stock

½ teaspoon salt

¼ teaspoon black pepper

Preheat oven to 425ºF.

In a large sauté pan over medium heat, heat the oil and sauté the leeks, celery, and garlic until soft. Mix in the corn bread, bay leaf, thyme, sage, pecans, and stock. Season with the salt and black pepper and bake until golden brown, about 20 minutes. Discard the bay leaf.

Wild Rice and Bread Stuffing

PREP TIME: 15 MINUTES   **COOK TIME:** 1 HOUR AND 20 MINUTES
SERVES 4 TO 6

There isn't a soul who will be able to tell that this is a vegan, gluten-free holiday dish. Actually, forget holiday—make it anytime the mood for stuffing strikes!

½ cup wild rice

3 cups low-sodium vegetable stock
    or water

2 tablespoons olive oil

1½ cups sliced, well-washed leeks

½ cup diced peeled carrot

½ cup diced celery

1 clove garlic, minced

1 bay leaf

3 cups 1-inch cubes gluten-free bread
    (about 10 slices)

1 tablespoon chopped fresh rosemary

1 tablespoon chopped fresh thyme

1 tablespoon chopped fresh sage

½ teaspoon salt

¼ teaspoon black pepper

½ cup dried or fresh cranberries
    (optional)

Preheat oven to 425°F.

In a small saucepot, combine the rice with 2 cups of the stock or water. Bring to a simmer over medium heat. Cover and cook for 45 minutes, or until the rice is tender. Set aside.

In a large sauté pan, heat the oil over medium heat and sauté the leeks, carrot, celery, garlic, and bay leaf until the vegetables are soft but not beginning to brown. Mix in the cooked rice, bread, herbs, salt, black pepper, cranberries, if using, and the remaining 1 cup stock or water. Bake in the oven for 25 minutes, or until golden brown. Discard the bay leaf.

BEANS, LEGUMES, AND PROTEIN

Bean and lentil dishes make the kind of warm, hearty, belly-filling meals that are just the thing when the weather gets cooler. But when chilled they can be tossed with some dressing for a quick and robust summer salad. Either way, because they're loaded with protein, they'll fill you up without weighing you down. Just be mindful that canned beans can have a lot of added sodium, so buy a lower-sodium brand and rinse them before cooking, or use dried, which is what I prefer.

As for protein substitutes like tofu and seitan, think of them as special treats for scratching the meat itch. When you just need to sink your teeth into something a little more substantial, these foods can really hit the spot.

Chickpeas and Spinach

PREP TIME: 10 MINUTES, PLUS OVERNIGHT SOAKING   COOK TIME: 30 MINUTES TO 2 HOURS
SERVES 4

2 cups dried chickpeas, soaked
  overnight and drained OR 3 (15-
  ounce) cans chickpeas, strained
  and liquid reserved
6 cups water (if using canned beans,
  reduce liquid to 4 cups)
¼ small onion, chopped
½ carrot, peeled and chopped

½ celery heart, chopped
¾ teaspoon salt
1 bay leaf
½ teaspoon cumin seeds
2 cloves garlic, peeled
¼ teaspoon black pepper
1 bunch well-rinsed spinach leaves
  (about 3 cups)

If using dried beans: Place the beans, the 6 cups water, the vegetables, ½ teaspoon of the salt, and the bay leaf in a large pot and bring to a boil. Reduce to a simmer and cook until the beans are tender, about 1½ hours. Skim off any foam that forms on the surface.

If using canned beans: Place the beans, reserved liquid, 4 cups water, vegetables, ½ teaspoon of the salt, and the bay leaf in a large pot and bring to a boil. Reduce to a simmer and cook until tender, about 15 minutes.

Remove and discard the bay leaf and strain the beans, reserving the cooking liquid.

In a blender, combine half the cooked chickpea mixture with the remaining chickpeas and their cooking liquid, and ¼ teaspoon salt, cumin seeds, garlic, and black pepper. Puree until smooth and velvety, using cooking liquid as needed.

Return the blender contents to the pot and bring to a simmer over medium heat. Add the spinach and serve.

White Beans and Escarole

PREP TIME: 10 MINUTES **COOK TIME:** 25 MINUTES
SERVES 4

2 tablespoons olive oil

2 cloves garlic, sliced

1 small onion, diced

2 (15-ounce) cans cannellini beans, strained, liquid reserved, and rinsed

1 tablespoon fresh thyme leaves

1 bay leaf

¼ teaspoon red pepper flakes

¼ teaspoon salt

¼ teaspoon black pepper

3 cups escarole, coarsely chopped

Heat the oil in a large pot over medium heat. Add the garlic and onion and sauté until translucent, but do not brown. Add the beans along with the thyme, bay leaf, and red pepper flakes. Season with the salt and black pepper. Simmer over medium-low heat for 15 minutes. Add the escarole and stir until wilted, about 5 minutes. Discard the bay leaf.

Red Lentil Daal

PREP TIME: 10 MINUTES   COOK TIME: 40 MINUTES
SERVES 4

Lentils are the most approachable members of the legume family because they don't have to be soaked overnight and take almost no time to cook. They come in a variety of colors, all of which have their own subtle flavor, and are just as delicious warm as they are cold. Both this dish with its intoxicating Indian spices and the French Lentils with Sherry Vinegar (page 207) can transform a bed of lettuce into a deeply satisfying lunch, dinner, or side dish.

¼ teaspoon fennel seeds

¼ teaspoon cumin seeds

¼ teaspoon mustard seeds

1 tablespoon olive oil

1 small onion, chopped

2 cloves garlic, chopped

½-inch piece of fresh ginger, peeled
and chopped

Pinch of red pepper flakes

1 teaspoon curry powder

¼ teaspoon turmeric

2 cups red lentils
(yellow lentils will
work here too)

½ teaspoon salt

¼ teaspoon black pepper

5 cups water

In a spice grinder or with a mortar and pestle, grind the fennel, cumin, and mustard seeds (already ground spices can be substituted).

Heat the oil in a large pot over medium-high heat. Add the onion, garlic, and ginger and sauté until soft and beginning to brown. Add the spice mixture, red pepper flakes, curry powder, and turmeric and let toast until fragrant, 1 to 2 minutes. Add the lentils, salt, black pepper, and water and simmer until the lentils are completely soft. Serve warm or at room temperature.

French Lentils with Sherry Vinegar

PREP TIME: 15 MINUTES   **COOK TIME:** 1 HOUR
SERVES 4

2½ tablespoons olive oil

1 cup ¼-inch-thick slices well-washed leeks

2 cloves garlic, minced

1 cup ¼-inch-thick slices peeled carrots

1 cup ¼-inch-thick slices celery

1 bay leaf

2 teaspoons salt

¼ teaspoon black pepper

2 cups French lentils (green or red will work here too)

1 tablespoon chopped fresh rosemary

3½ cups water or low-sodium vegetable stock

¼ cup red wine

3 tablespoons sherry vinegar

½ cup dried cranberries

½ cup chopped walnuts

¼ cup chopped fresh parsley

In a large soup pot, heat the oil over medium heat. Add the leeks, garlic, carrots, celery, and bay leaf and sauté until leeks and garlic are translucent, about 4 minutes. Season with the salt and black pepper.

Add the lentils, rosemary, water or stock, and wine. Bring to a boil, reduce to a simmer, and cover. Cook for 40 minutes. Add the vinegar and continue cooking if the lentils are not already tender.

Remove from the heat and add the cranberries, walnuts, and parsley. Cover and leave for 5 minutes while the cranberries rehydrate. Discard the bay leaf. Serve.

Seitan Bo Ssam

PREP TIME: 20 MINUTES, PLUS 4 HOURS TO OVERNIGHT FOR MARINATING
COOK TIME: 20 MINUTES
SERVES 4

You can have a lot of fun with seitan because when it's grilled or sautéed, you get the same smoky, caramelized flavor and texture as meat. It needs a little boost in the flavor department, so marinating goes a long way, but once it's infused with these classic Asian flavors and smothered with Sesame-Scallion Dressing (page 210), it's a spot-on impersonation of traditional Korean lettuce wraps. It also doesn't hurt that when it's heaped with spicy kimchi—fermented cabbage—you're getting all the digestive benefits of probiotics, but your family will think it's just really tasty finger food.

8 ounces seitan, drained and cut into
    2-inch pieces

2 tablespoons soy sauce or Bragg Liquid Aminos

1 apple, juiced, or ¼ cup apple juice

2 cloves garlic, smashed

½ onion, coarsely chopped

¼ teaspoon black pepper

½ teaspoon sesame oil

1½ tablespoons peanut oil (if using a pan)

1 head Boston or Bibb lettuce, separated
    into individual leaves

1 recipe Basic Brown Rice (page 193)

1 (16-ounce) jar kimchi

Sesame-Scallion Dressing (recipe follows)

Mix the seitan, soy sauce or liquid aminos, apple juice, garlic, onion, black pepper, and sesame oil together in a bowl. Cover and allow to marinate 4 hours or overnight, stirring periodically to make sure all the seitan is submerged. Remove the seitan from the marinade and blot dry with a paper towel.

Heat a grill over a medium-high flame, or heat a grill pan or sauté pan over medium-high heat and add the peanut oil, allowing it to get hot. Add the seitan. Cook until it gets brown and crispy on one side, 3 to 5 minutes. Flip over and repeat. Remove and place in a serving bowl.

Use a lettuce leaf as a cup and make a small bed of brown rice in it. Top with the seitan, kimchi, and dressing.

Sesame-Scallion Dressing

PREP TIME: 5 MINUTES   **COOK TIME:** 10 MINUTES
MAKES 1 CUP

2 tablespoons sesame seeds

1 tablespoon plus 1 teaspoon peanut oil

4 scallions, whites and greens, chopped

1-inch piece fresh ginger, peeled
  and minced

3 cloves garlic, minced

¼ teaspoon red pepper flakes

3 tablespoons mirin

¼ cup soy sauce or Bragg Liquid
  Aminos

½ tablespoon miso dissolved in
  ¼ cup warm water

In a small dry pan, heat the sesame seeds over low heat until fragrant and lightly browned, about 2 minutes. Reserve.

In a small pot, heat the oil over medium heat. Add the scallions, ginger, and garlic and cook until they become aromatic, being careful not to burn them, for 2 minutes. Add the red pepper flakes, mirin, soy sauce or liquid aminos, and miso-water mixture and simmer for 5 minutes. Remove from the heat and add the sesame seeds.

Scallion-Tomato Tofu Scramble

PREP TIME: 10 MINUTES   **COOK TIME:** 10 MINUTES
SERVES 4

There are days when a juice or a bowl of rice and vegetables will do the trick for breakfast, and then there are days when you might need to call in the big guns. For something truly hearty in the morning, this omelet stand-in does the trick. The turmeric gives the tofu a deeper, earthier flavor while turning it egg yolk–gold in color.

1 tablespoon olive oil

3 scallions, chopped

1 clove garlic, minced

1 pound firm tofu, drained and cut into
   1-inch cubes

½ teaspoon salt

¼ teaspoon black pepper

¼ teaspoon turmeric

½ cup chopped seeded tomatoes

Heat a medium-size sauté pan over medium-high heat. Add the oil, scallions, and garlic and cook until aromatic, about 2 minutes. Add the tofu, breaking up the cubes slightly as they cook. Season with the salt, black pepper, and turmeric. Stir in the tomatoes, heat until just warm, and serve.

SOMETHING SWEET

Wine-Poached Pears with Saffron, Apricots, and Almonds

PREP TIME: 10 MINUTES   **COOK TIME:** 35 MINUTES
SERVES 8

I can't say enough about this exceptionally sophisticated, simply gorgeous dessert. Gently bathing the pears in an aromatic Jacuzzi takes them to a place where very few fruits have gone. Their soft, spiced flesh is just as good chilled as it is warm, making this dish appropriate for any season—though I think it makes a lovely addition to a holiday table.

> *Note:* You can use red wine or port in the poaching liquid. Just omit the saffron and, in the case of port, halve the honey. Apples can also be substituted for pears.

½ vanilla bean

4 pears, peeled, halved, stems intact

4 cups water

1 cup white wine or sparkling wine such as *cava* or *prosecco*

1 cinnamon stick

Pinch of saffron

2 tablespoons honey

1 cup apricots, dried or pitted fresh, cut into thirds

½ cup sliced almonds, toasted

Split the vanilla bean lengthwise and run the tip of your knife or a spoon down the inside to collect the seeds. Reserve.

Using a melon baller or teaspoon, remove the seeds from the inside of the pears.

In a large saucepot, combine the water, wine, vanilla pod and seeds, cinnamon, saffron, and honey. Bring to a boil, then reduce to a simmer and cook for 5 minutes. Gently slide the pears into the poaching liquid and simmer until a knife can be inserted but still can meet resistance, 15 to 20 minutes. Remove from the heat and allow the pears to cool in the poaching liquid.

Carefully remove the pears and reserve. Return the poaching liquid to a boil, having removed the vanilla bean and cinnamon stick, and reduce until syrupy in consistency. Add the apricots and heat for another minute. Place the pears in individual bowls and smother them in sauce and apricots. Sprinkle with the almonds and serve.

Tapioca Pudding

PREP TIME: 35 MINUTES   **COOK TIME:** 25 MINUTES
SERVES 4

I was a big fan of tapioca pudding when I was a little girl. There's just something about it that's so comforting. I wondered if it might make a good vegan dessert, and lo and behold, it does! Be sure to taste as you add the sweetener; the amount you need will differ depending on which you use.

- ¼ cup plus 2 tablespoons tapioca pearls
- 4 cups water
- 1⅓ cups almond milk
- ¼ teaspoon salt
- ⅓ cup grated unsweetened coconut
- ¼ cup stevia, maple syrup, or brown rice syrup

In a medium-size saucepot, soak the tapioca in the water for 30 minutes.

Add the almond milk and salt, and over medium-high heat bring the mixture to a boil, stirring frequently to keep the tapioca pearls from forming lumps. Reduce the heat to low and simmer for 5 more minutes.

Add the coconut and sweetener and simmer 10 more minutes, continuing to stir occasionally.

Remove from the heat, pour into a shallow container, and chill until set.

Chocolate Coconut Mousse

PREP TIME: 5 MINUTES   **COOK TIME:** 10 MINUTES
SERVES 10

Airy and light yet rich on the tongue, this mousse always flies under the radar of those who think they know a vegan dessert when they see one. Heap it in bowls or layer it in a glass with bananas and strawberries for a parfait—either way, you'll be hard-pressed to put the spoon down.

¼ cup plus 2 tablespoons almond milk

8 ounces good dark chocolate, chopped

8 ounces silken tofu

1 (15-ounce) can coconut milk

In a small pot, warm the almond milk over medium heat until it just begins to steam. Remove from the heat and add the chocolate, stirring to melt. Return to the heat if necessary to help it along. Cool slightly.

Add the milk mixture, tofu, and coconut milk to a blender and process until smooth. Transfer to a bowl or serving glasses and chill for 3 to 4 hours, until set.

Pumpkin Pie with Pecan Crust

PREP TIME: 25 MINUTES   **COOK TIME:** 1 HOUR AND 15 MINUTES
MAKES ONE 9-INCH PIE

Need I say more?

PECAN CRUST

2½ cups pecans

3 tablespoons vegetable spread, such as Earth Balance, melted

PIE FILLING

1 cup raw cashews, soaked in 1½ cups water for 1 hour

2 tablespoons egg replacer

2 (15-ounce) cans pumpkin puree

½ teaspoon ground cinnamon

¼ teaspoon ground nutmeg

¼ teaspoon ground allspice

¼ cup maple syrup

Place the pecans in a food processor and pulse until they're crumb-size. Be careful not to overprocess to a paste. Transfer to a small mixing bowl and stir in the vegetable spread until the mixture is evenly combined. Press the crumbs into a 9-inch springform pan, covering the bottom completely and having a 1-inch rise on the sides. Place the pan in the refrigerator and allow the crust to chill as you make the filling.

Preheat oven to 325°F.

Place the cashews, ½ cup plus 3 tablespoons soaking liquid, and the egg replacer in a blender or food processor and puree until smooth. Add the pumpkin puree, spices, and maple syrup and blend again until smooth.

Pour the filling into the prepared crust, spreading evenly in the pan.

Bake until the top of the pie begins to caramelize, 45 to 50 minutes. Remove from the oven and let cool completely. Refrigerate the pie for at least 4 hours so the filling can set. Remove from the pan and slice.

Stewed Apples with Crushed Mixed Nuts

To me, nothing speaks of fall like apples and cider. This dish will make your house smell like autumn.

½ cup fresh orange juice

½ cup apple cider

1 vanilla bean, split and seeds scraped (see page 213), or
    1 teaspoon vanilla extract

¼ teaspoon ground nutmeg

1 cinnamon stick (can substitute 1 teaspoon ground cinnamon)

4 apples, peeled, cored, and cut into 1-inch pieces

1 pear, peeled, cored, and cut into 1-inch pieces

1 cup green grapes, halved

1 cup mixed nuts, crushed

Bring the orange juice, cider, vanilla bean, nutmeg, and cinnamon to a simmer in a large saucepot. Add the apples and pear and cook, stirring frequently, until just tender, about 15 minutes. Be careful not to overcook or the fruit will become mushy. Remove from the heat and discard the vanilla bean and the cinnamon stick. Stir in the grapes and nuts. Serve warm or cold.

Fruity Freezer Pops

PREP TIME: 10 MINUTES

SERVES 12

These cold treats are ridiculously good. Their intense fruit flavor is better than any Popsicle I've ever bought in a store, and because they make the perfect afternoon craft for kids, winning the ice-cream truck battle just got a whole lot easier.

2 cups hulled strawberries, fresh or frozen

3 cups coarsely chopped peeled mango, fresh (about
     2 mangoes) or frozen

Place the fruit in a blender and process until smooth. Pass through a fine-mesh strainer into a pitcher, pour into molds, and freeze.

Almond-Milk Chai Tea

PREP TIME: 5 MINUTES   **COOK TIME:** 45 MINUTES
SERVES 6

This warm, spiced drink is a lovely way to end a meal on a sweet note. Serve it to guests instead of coffee, and it makes the house smell festive and inviting. It's also the perfect antidote to a Starbucks addiction.

Have patience when making this—the flavors really come forward as it steeps.

6 cups water

1-inch piece fresh ginger, peeled and sliced

7 cardamom pods

7 whole cloves

1 cinnamon stick

4 tea bags Darjeeling or chamomile tea (caffeine-free)

3 cups almond milk

½ cup maple syrup

To a large pot add the water, ginger, cardamom, cloves, and cinnamon and bring to a boil. Reduce the heat and simmer for 30 minutes. Remove from the heat, add the tea bags, and steep for 10 minutes. Remove the tea bags. Add the almond milk and maple syrup and heat until warm, strain, then serve.

Iced Tea with Honey and Mint

PREP TIME: 5 MINUTES   **COOK TIME:** 15 MINUTES
SERVES 4

Sometimes cooking inspiration comes from something as simple as having spare ingredients lying around. Christopher saw a huge bunch of mint in my fridge and said, "We can make tea!"

You can drink this warm or iced, and while it's tasty enough for everyday drinking, it's also perfect to sip during a detox. Fresh mint calms the stomach, aids digestion, and helps flush bad bacteria out of your system.

8 cups water

2 tablespoons honey

2 cups fresh mint leaves, loosely packed

Juice of 1 lemon

3 cups ice

In a large saucepot over high heat, bring the water to a boil. Stir in the honey and remove from the heat. Add the mint and let steep for 5 minutes. Add the lemon juice and 2 cups of the ice. Once the tea has cooled, fill the glasses with the remaining 1 cup ice and serve. Or, omit the ice and serve warm.

> **VARIATION:** You can also make this tea in the sun by combining the water, honey, and mint together in a large pitcher or jar and leaving it in a sunny spot for 4 hours. Add the lemon juice and serve over ice.

Special Menus

THE HOLIDAY TABLE

Mashed Potatoes with
Wild Mushroom Gravy

Candied Sweet Potatoes with Apples

Wild Rice and Bread Stuffing

Warm Haricot Verts Salad
with Butter Beans, Hazelnuts,
and Curry Vinaigrette

Pumpkin Pie with Pecan Crust

SUMMER COOKOUT

Iced Tea with Honey and Mint

Corn Bread

Purple Potato Salad with
Whole-Grain Mustard

Grilled Portabella Mushrooms

Fruity Freezer Pops

ACKNOWLEDGMENTS

My journey, and as a result this book, could not have been what it was without the support and inspiration of many. I'd like to offer special thanks to:

Dr. Roni DeLuz, James Hester, Sara Soulati, John Salley, Natalia Rose, Gil Jacobs, and the We Care Spa, for showing me the path to health and changing my life.

Dr. Jed Kaminetsky, for being my advocate.

Dr. David Agus, for guiding me through this recent journey and being a friend.

Dr. Leslie Boyd, Dr. Elliot Newman, Dr. Mark Lemert, Dr. Edward Greaney, and the staff at NYU Medical Center, the team that got me through this.

Joy Pierson at the Candle Café, for proving that delicious and healthy are not mutually exclusive.

Howard Stern, Gary Dell'Abate, Fred Norris, Tim Sabean, Mel Karmazin, and the Sirius family, for all your love and encouragement.

Jody Dunowitz, friend in veganism, who has followed me on this journey.

Don Buchwald, my teacher, my guide, and the best agent on Earth. And Laura Buchwald, for your guidance and support.

My collaborator, Rachel Holtzman, for helping me put my heart on the page.

Dennis Feeley, for making my life so much easier and for introducing me to Christopher Sanchez.

Christopher Sanchez, for teaching me how gorgeous vegetables can be and bestowing my title of Queen of the Grill Pan.

Tara Donne and Martha Bernabe, for making this book so delectably beautiful.

My editor, Megan Newman, for her wise vision, and the rest of the Penguin team: William Shinker, Lisa Johnson, Andrea Ho, Nellys Li, Richard Basch, and Gigi Campo.

All my fans, who have joined me in my adventures.

My family, for teaching me how powerful our choices are.

My nephew, Anthony Quivers, for listening!

APPENDIX A:
KITCHEN BASICS

Measuring spoons

Measuring cups

Cutting board

Peeler

Zester

Grater

Citrus reamer

Heat-resistant spatula

Wooden spoon

Slotted/perforated metal spoon

4-ounce and 8-ounce ladles

Metal spatula

Mandoline

Colander

Fine-mesh strainer

Set of mixing bowls

Digital food scale

Whisk

Salad spinner

Tongs

Oven mitts

Can opener

Manual knife sharpener

Baking sheet

Knives

    6-inch chef's knife

    4-inch utility knife

    paring knife

    large serrated knife

Pots and pans

    heavy-bottomed, oven-safe
      stew pot

    8-quart saucepot

    2-quart saucepot

    8-inch, 10-inch, and 12-inch
      sauté pans

    10-inch grill pan

Equipment

    juicer

    blender

    food processor

    rice cooker

APPENDIX B:
SEASONAL FRUITS
AND VEGETABLES

SPRING

Asparagus

Bok choy

Broccoli rabe

English peas

Escarole

Fiddleheads

Garlic

Garlic scapes

Green garlic

Lettuces such as romaine,
  butterhead, mesclun mix,
  dandelion greens

Nettles

Onions

Radicchio

Radishes

Ramps

Rhubarb

Sorrel

Spinach

Spring leeks

Spring onions

Sunchokes

Watercress

Wild mushrooms

SUMMER

Apricots

Artichokes

Blackberries

Blueberries

Broccoli

Cabbages

Cardoons

Carrots

Cauliflower

Cherries

Corn

Cucumbers

Currants

Eggplants

Fava beans

Fennel

Garlic

Green beans

Kohlrabi

Lima beans

Melons

Mushrooms

Nectarines

Okra

Onions

Peaches

Pears

Peppers

Plums

Raspberries

Salad greens

Strawberries

Summer squashes

Tomatillos

Tomatoes

Zucchini

FALL

Apples

Asian pears

Bok choy

Broccoli

Broccoli rabe

Brussels sprouts

Cabbages

Carrots

Cauliflower

Celery

Celery root

Collard greens

Cranberries

Edamame

Endive

Escarole

Fennel

Garlic

Ginger

Grapes

Kale

Leeks

Mushrooms

Mustard greens

Onions

Pumpkins

Quinces

Rutabagas

Salsify

Shallots

Spinach
Sunchokes
Sweet potatoes

Turnips
Winter squashes

WINTER

Brussels sprouts
Cabbages
Carrots
Cauliflower
Celery root
Endive
Garlic
Leeks
Onions

Parsnips
Pumpkins
Radicchio
Rutabagas
Sweet potatoes
West Coast citrus
Winter squashes
Yams

APPENDIX C:
COOKING METHODS

EAT IT RAW

Broccoli

Cabbages

Carrots

Cauliflower

Corn

Endive

Fennel

Leeks

Onions

Peas

Radicchio

Radishes

Shallots

Summer squashes

Zucchini

GRILL IT

Asparagus

Broccoli rabe

Corn

Eggplants

Leeks

Mushrooms

Onions

Peppers

Romaine

Summer squashes

Tomatoes

Zucchini

ROAST IT

Asparagus

Beets

Broccoli

Brussels sprouts

Carrots

Cauliflower

Celery root

Eggplants

Fennel

Leeks

Mushrooms

Parsnips

Peppers

Rutabagas

Shallots

Sunchokes

Sweet potatoes

Winter squashes

Zucchini

SAUTÉ IT

Bok choy

Broccoli

Broccoli rabe

Brussels sprouts

Cabbages

Collards

Eggplants

Green beans

Kale

Leeks

Mushrooms

Okra

Onions

Peas

Shallots

Spinach

Summer squashes

Swiss chard

Zucchini

STEAM IT

Asparagus

Bok choy

Broccoli rabe

Cabbages

Collards

Green beans

Kale

Peas

Spinach

Summer squashes

Swiss chard

APPENDIX D:
HERBS AND SPICES

ASIAN

Basil

Chinese chives

Five-spice powder*

Garlic

Ginger

Lemongrass

Mint

Red and black peppercorns

Red and green chilies

Sesame seeds

Star anise

FRENCH

Chervil

Chives

Marjoram

Parsley

Rosemary

Sage

Tarragon

Thyme

INDIAN

Black peppercorns

Cardamom pods

Chaat masala*

Cinnamon

---

*Spice blends that you usually find premade.

Cloves

Coriander

Cumin

Curry powder*

Garam masala*

Ground ginger

Ground nutmeg

Mustard seeds

Red chilies

Turmeric

ITALIAN

Basil

Bay leaves

Fennel seeds

Garlic

Oregano

Parsley

Rosemary

Sage

MEXICAN

Cayenne pepper

Coriander

Cumin

Garlic powder

Ground ancho pepper

Oregano

---

*Spice blends that you usually find premade.

NOTES

Chapter 2. Fat and Sick Is Not Your Destiny

Page 14. *some natural event that just* happens: T. Colin Campbell, PhD, and Thomas M. Campbell II, MD, *The China Study* (Dallas: BenBella Books, Inc., 2006), 13.

Page 14. *we just have to live with it:* ibid., 225–26.

Page 15. *your genetics don't make heart disease inevitable:* ibid., 233.

Chapter 3. You Are What You Eat and Can't Excrete

Page 21. *This function helps us deal with changes:* Karen E. Jensen, "Homeostasis," Biology Reference. www.biologyreference.com/Gr-Hi/Health.html#b

Page 22. *A steak can take up to three days to digest:* Dr. Mehmet Oz, "How Long Does It Take Food to Digest?" Oprah.com. www.oprah.com/health/Facing-the-FAQs/1

Page 26. *have their hands deep in the medical education system:* Brad Kava, "How Much Does Your Doctor Take from Drug Companies?" Redwood City Patch, last modified January 26, 2012. http://redwoodcity.patch.com/articles/how-much-does-your-doctor-take-from-drug-companies-cd163477

Page 26. *minimal amount of education on nutrition:* Kelly M. Adams, MPH, RD, Martin Kohlmeier, MD, Steven H. Zeisel, MD, PhD, "Nutrition Education in U.S. Medical Schools: Latest Update of a National Survey," *Academic Medicine* 85, no. 9 (2010): 1537–42. doi: 10.1097/ACM.0b013e3181eab71b

Page 26. *doctors don't know everything:* Mayrav Saar, "What Your Doctor Doesn't Tell You," *New York Post,* last modified February 5, 2012. www.nypost.com/p/news/opinion/opedcolumnists/what_your_doctor_doesn_tell_you_RGm6oJpm2eUOsJj89c3JJO

Page 27. *doesn't significantly reduce your risk for heart attack or stroke:* NHS Choices, "Study Finds Daily Aspirin 'Harmful,'" last modified September 1, 2009. www.nhs.uk/news/2009/08August/Pages/Studyfindsdailyaspirinharmful.aspx

Page 27. *tests and predictors can only guesstimate:* David S. Martin, "Will You Have a Heart Attack? These Tests Might Tell," CNN Health, last modified August 26, 2011. www.cnn.com/2011/HEALTH/08/16/tests.picture.heart.attack/index.html

Chapter 4. Meat, Dairy, and Processed Food

Page 31. *According to the World Health Organization:* Fossette Allane, "What Percentage of Diseases Are Linked to the Diet?" Livestrong.com, last updated October 3, 2011. www.livestrong.com/article/545669-what-percentage-of-diseases-are-linked-to-the-diet

Page 32. *increasing the acidity in your system:* Dr. Donald L. Hayes, DC, "pH Balancing May Help Ease Muscle & Joint Pain Naturally," *Practice Insights.* www.greensfirst.com/gestion/pHBalancingMuscleJointPain%20Articl.pdf

Page 32. *Inflammation is basically your body misfiring:* Shara Yurkiewicz, "Battling Inflammation, Disease Through Food," *Los Angeles Times,* last updated August 17, 2009. http://articles.latimes.com/2009/aug/17/health/he-anti-inflammation17

Page 32. *80 percent higher risk of developing Alzheimer's and dementia:* W. L. Xu, MD, PhD, A. R. Atti, MD, PhD, M. Gatz, PhD, N. L. Pedersen, PhD, B. Johansson, PhD, and L. Fratiglioni, MD, PhD, "Midlife Overweight and Obesity Increase Late-Life Dementia Risk," *Neurology* 76, no. 18 (2011): 1568–74. doi:10.1212/WNL.0b013e3182190d09

Page 33. *factory farms are really just huge expanses of crowded animals:* Environmental Protection Agency, *Producers' Compliance Guide for CAFOs,* August 2003.

Page 33. *where 99 percent of all meat raised and slaughtered in the US comes from:* Calculation based on US Department of Agriculture, *2002 Census of Agriculture,* June 2004. Farm Forward, "Factory Farming." www.farmforward.com/farming-forward/factory-farming

Page 34. *released a video they shot undercover:* Huffington Post, "Kreider Egg Farms Video from Humane Society Uncovers Horrible Chicken Abuse," last updated April 12, 2012. www.huffingtonpost.com/2012/04/12/kreider-egg-farms-video_n_1420585.html

Page 35. *feeding the cows "organic" high-fructose corn syrup:* Michael Pollan, *The Omnivore's Dilemma* (New York: Penguin, 2006), 139.

Page 36. *processed foods are contrived to be as attractive to consumers as possible:* David A. Kessler, MD, *The End of Overeating* (New York: Rodale, 2009), 115.

Page 36. *suckers and addicts when it comes to sugar and fat:* ibid., 14.

Page 36. *our brains adapted to reward us:* ibid., 10.

Page 36. *incentive to go out and hunt for the foods that did us the most good:* ibid., 84.

Page 36. *as difficult to resist as the drugs themselves:* Anna Deschamps, "Scientific Research Linking High Sugar Processed Foods to Addictions Like Cocaine," The Random Fact, last updated November 3, 2011. http://therandomfact.com/scientific-research-linking-high-sugar-processed-foods-to-addictions-like-cocaine/2210344

Page 36. *Companies in charge of selling us food:* Kessler, *Overeating,* 14.

Page 37. *the more sugar and fat we eat, the more sugar and fat we crave:* ibid.

Page 37. *created so that they're easier to chew and swallow:* ibid., 69.

Page 37. *calories from sugar are different than calories from other foods: 60 Minutes* interview with Robert H. Lustig, MD, April 1, 2012.

Page 37. *carry virtually no nutritional benefits:* Michael Pollan, *Food Rules* (New York: Penguin, 2009), 81.

Page 38. *roller-coaster ride that taxes all your systems:* Jessica Porter, *The Hip Chick's Guide to Macrobiotics* (New York: Avery, 2004), 126–27.

Page 38. *resulting in type 2 diabetes:* ibid.

Page 38. *the more acidic your blood becomes:* ibid.

Page 38. *cancers have figured out a way to benefit:* 60 Minutes interview with Lewis C. Cantley, PhD, April 1, 2012.

Page 38. *liver gets overloaded with sugar:* 60 Minutes interview with Lustig.

Page 39. *good at clogging arteries and causing heart attacks:* ibid.

Page 39. *subjects who went from a healthy diet:* 60 Minutes interview with Kimber Stanhope, PhD, MS, April 1, 2012.

Page 39. *Current wisdom dictates:* Val Willingham, "Federal Dietary Guidelines Target Salt, Saturated Fats," CNN Health, last updated February 1, 2011. www.cnn.com/2011/HEALTH/01/31/dietary.guildelines/index.html

Page 39. *It's not just the obvious offenders like chips and pretzels:* WebMD, "Salt Shockers Slideshow." www.webmd.com/diet/ss/slideshow-salt-shockers

Page 40. *has been linked to a familiar litany of offenses:* Nicholas Bakalar, "Risks: Diet Soft Drinks Linked to Heart Disease," *The New York Times,* last updated February 27, 2012. www.nytimes.com/2012/02/28/health/research/diet-soft-drinks-linked-to-risk-of-heart-disease.html

Page 40. *the following warning on Sweet'N Low packets:* Roni DeLuz, RN, ND, PhD, and James Hester, *21 Pounds in 21 Days* (New York: Harper, 2007), 49.

Page 41. *Better Sugar Substitutes:* Porter, *Hip Chick's Guide,* 126–27.

Chapter 5. Plants

Page 44. *getting all the vitamins, minerals, and nutrients that you need:* T. Colin Campbell, PhD, and Thomas M. Campbell II, MD, *The China Study* (Dallas: BenBella Books, Inc., 2006), 48.

Page 45. *most protection possible by eating a wide variety of fruits and vegetables:* ibid., 93.

Page 45. *Plants give us the power of fiber:* ibid., 89–90.

Page 46. *Plants make you skinny:* ibid., 101.

Page 46. *you'll feel fuller longer:* ibid., 98.

Page 46. *you most likely don't need to take a vitamin supplement:* Michael Pollan, *Food Rules* (New York: Penguin, 2009), 87.

Page 46. *complex biochemical system involving thousands of components:* Campbell and Campbell, *China Study,* 228–29.

Page 47. *The two main exceptions:* ibid., 242.

Page 47. *A deficiency in B_{12}:* Victor Herbert, MD, JD, "Vitamin B-12: Plant Sources, Requirements, and Assay," *The American Journal of Clinical Nutrition* 48 (1988): 852–58.

Chapter 6. Kick It Off with a Detox

Page 53. *You're giving it space to purge all the toxins:* Roni DeLuz, RN, ND, PhD, and James Hester, *21 Pounds in 21 Days* (New York: Harper, 2007), 90; Shari Roan, "Running on Empty: The Pros and Cons of Fasting," *Los Angeles Times,* last updated February 2, 2009. http://articles.latimes.com/2009/feb/02/health/he-fasting2

Page 53. *can start to mend themselves:* DeLuz and Hester, 102.

Page 55. *there's no going to the refrigerator when you're starving:* Patti Neighmond, "Weight-Loss Surgery: It's Not for Everyone," NPR, last updated August 17, 2006. www.npr.org/templates/story/story.php ?storyId=5658690

Chapter 7. Making Friends with Food

Page 69. *It takes twenty minutes for your brain to realize that your body is eating:* Christa Miller, "How Long Does It Take Your Brain to Register That the Stomach Is Full?" Livestrong.com, last updated June 27, 2011. www.livestrong.com/article/480254-how-long-does-it-take-your-brain-to-register-that-the-stomach-is -full/#ixzz1tACnY6xg

Page 70. *estimated advertising expenditure for restaurants and for food, beverage, and candy companies:* Consumers Union, "New Report Shows Food Industry Advertising Overwhelms Government's '5 A Day' Campaign to Fight Obesity and Promote Healthy Eating," last updated September 13, 2005. www.consumersunion .org/pub/core_health_care/002657.html

Page 71. *A 2010 study:* Paul M. Johnson and Paul J. Kenny, "Dopamine D2 Receptors in Addiction-Like Reward Dysfunction and Compulsive Eating in Obese Rats," *Nature Neuroscience* 13 (2010): 635–41. doi:10.1038/nn.2519

Page 73. *the worse it is for your health:* Nicholas Bakalar, "Risks: More Red Meat, More Mortality," *The New York Times,* last updated March 12, 2012. www.nytimes.com/2012/03/13/health/research/red-meat -linked-to-cancer-and-heart-disease.html

Page 74. *stopped using ammonium hydroxide in the production of their meat:* Alissa Skelton, "Internet Users Flock to Google Search to Learn About 'Pink Slime,'" Mashables, last updated March 9, 2012. http://mashable .com/2012/03/09/pink-slime-google-search-trending

Page 75. *any other lifestyle or environmental factor, including tobacco use and car accidents:* T. Colin Campbell, PhD, and Thomas M. Campbell II, MD, *The China Study* (Dallas: BenBella Books, Inc., 2006), 305–7.

Page 75. *Take, for instance, a panel for the Food and Nutrition Board:* ibid., 289–90.

Page 76. *allowing tomato paste on pizzas in school lunches to be counted as a vegetable:* "Tomato Sauce on Pizza is a Vegetable, says Congress," *New York Daily News,* last updated November 16, 2011. http://articles .nydailynews.com/2011-11-16/news/30407819_1_school-lunch-pizza-tomato-paste

Page 77. *the best nutritional pedigree:* Karl Weber, ed., *Food, Inc.* (New York: PublicAffairs, 2009), 56.

Page 77. *only way to guard yourself:* ibid., 80–81.

Page 77. *Organic produce is better for your kids too:* ibid., 104.

Page 77. *Schlepping these things over land, sea, and air takes a ton of fuel:* Michael Pollan, *The Omnivore's Dilemma* (New York: Penguin, 2006), 183.

Chapter 8. Be Good to Yourself

Page 83. *Sitting around has also been linked:* Michelle Castillo, "Sitting Too Much May Double Your Risk of Dying Study Shows." CBS News, last updated March 27, 2012. http://www.cbsnews.com/8301-504763_162 -57405178-10391704/sitting-too-much-may-double-your-risk-of-dying-study-shows

Page 85. *Experts now believe:* David W. Freeman, "Too Much Sitting Behind 92,000 Cancer Cases a Year, Studies Report." http://www.cbsnews.com/8301-504763_162-57317789-10391704/too-much-sitting -behind-92000-cancer-cases-a-year-report/?tag=contentMain;contentBody

Page 88. *Researchers have discovered that eight hours:* National Sleep Foundation, "How Much Sleep Do We Really Need?" www.sleepfoundation.org/article/how-sleep-works/how-much-sleep-do-we-really-need

Page 88. *Find a Doctor Who Helps:* advice and insight in this section taken from an interview with Nikol Margiotta, DN, ABAAHP, FAAFRM, from the Raby Institute for Integrative Medicine at Northwestern.

Page 90. *insurance model is miserably outdated:* Dr. Sweeney, "Does My Health Insurance Cover Functional Medicine?" Last updated June 5, 2011. http://drsweeney.wordpress.com/2011/06/05/does-my-health-insurance-cover-functional-medicine

Page 91. *An Ounce of Prevention:* advice and insight in this section taken from an interview with Nikol Margiotta.

Page 92. *leg spasms that are exacerbated by exercise:* Gretchen Reynolds, "Do Statins Make It Tough to Exercise?" *The New York Times,* last updated March 14, 2012. http://well.blogs.nytimes.com/2012/03/14/do-statins-make-it-tough-to-exercise

Chapter 11. Recipes

Page 144. *neither vegetables nor nutritious:* Ron Nixon, "School Lunch Proposals Set Off a Dispute," *The New York Times,* last updated November 1, 2011. www.nytimes.com/2011/11/02/us/school-lunch-proposals-set-off-a-dispute.html?pagewanted=all

Page 223. *Fresh mint calms the stomach:* Brenna Coleman, "Health Benefits of Mint Tea," Examiner.com, last updated June 8, 2009. www.examiner.com/article/health-benefits-of-mint-tea

INDEX

A

acidic foods, 32, 33, 38
addiction to food, 28–30,
    36–37, 71–72
aging, 13–15
Almond-Butter Peach
    Smoothie, 115
Almond-Milk Chai Tea, 222
almonds
    Chilled Couscous with
        Cucumber and Mint,
        198–99
    Wine-Poached Pears with
        Saffron, Apricots, and
        Almonds, 213–14
animal-based foods, 22,
    31–35, 73
apples
    Apple, Fennel, Kale
        Juice, 112

Candied Sweet Potatoes
    with Apples, 190
Carrot, Apple, Ginger
    Juice, 113
Seitan Bo Ssam, 209–10
Stewed Apples with
    Crushed Mixed
    Nuts, 220
Wine-Poached Pears with
    Saffron, Apricots, and
    Almonds (substitution),
    213–14
apricots
    Moroccan-Spiced Apricot
        Topping, 180
    Wine-Poached Pears with
        Saffron, Apricots, and
        Almonds, 213–14
Artichoke Hearts, Roasted,
    with Walnut-Arugula
    Pesto, 188–89

arugula
    Green Bean and Nicoise
        Olive Salad, 141
    Walnut-Arugula Pesto, 189
    Warm Chayote Squash
        Salad with Avocados
        and Arugula, 135
asparagus
    Eggplant or Asparagus
        "Takeout" with
        Chinese Garlic Sauce,
        170–71
    Roasted or Grilled
        Asparagus with
        Lemon, 150
avocados
    Avocado, Pineapple, Chili,
        Lime Smoothie, 116
    Chilled Soba Noodle Salad
        with Grilled Pineapple
        and Avocados, 142–43

avocados *(cont.)*
   to prepare, 142
   Warm Chayote Squash
      Salad with Avocados
      and Arugula, 135

B

bananas
   Green Smoothie, 116
   Peach Almond-Butter
      Smoothie, 115
BBQ Sauce, Tangy, 175
beans and legumes
   Chickpeas and Spinach, 204
   French Lentils with Sherry
      Vinegar, 207
   Garbanzo Bean Lemon-
      Dill Dressing, 139
   Garbanzo Bean
      Vinaigrette, 138
   Red Lentil Daal, 206
   White Beans and
      Escarole, 205
Beets, Roasted, and White
      Balsamic Vinegar, 159
bell peppers. *See* peppers
Better-Than-You've-Ever-Had
      Gazpacho, 130–31
beverages
   Almond-Milk Chai
      Tea, 222
   Apple, Fennel, Kale
      Juice, 112
   Avocado, Pineapple, Chili,
      Lime Smoothie, 116
   Carrot, Apple, Ginger
      Juice, 113

Cucumber, Celery, Spinach
      Juice, 112
   Green Leaf Juice, 113
   Green Smoothie, 116
   Iced Tea with Honey and
      Mint, 223
   Peach Almond-Butter
      Smoothie, 115
blood tests, 47, 91–93
Boston Bibb Salad with
      Pistachios, Meyer
      Lemon, and Cucumber
      Ribbons, 137
brain function
   food addiction, 29–30, 36,
      71–72
   plaque buildup, 32
   satiety, 69–70
Braised Parsnips, 146
Bread, Corn, 200
breakfast, 73
broccoli
   Roasted Broccoli au
      Gratin, 152
   Silky Broccoli Soup, 119
Broccoli Rabe with Garlic and
      Red Pepper Flakes, 157
Brown Rice, Basic, 193
Brussels Sprouts Two Ways
   Roasted Brussels Sprouts
      with Fresh Rosemary,
      155
   Sautéed Brussels Sprouts
      with White Miso and
      Sesame Seeds, 154
Butter Beans, Hazelnuts, and
      Curry Vinaigrette,
      Warm Haricot Verts
      Salad with, 140

Butternut Squash Soup
      Two Ways
   Marrakesh-Blend Squash
      Soup, 126
   Scarborough Fair Squash
      Soup, 125

C

Cabbage, Red Wine–Braised,
      156–57
Candied Sweet Potatoes with
      Apples, 190
Caponata, Eggplant, 184
carrots
   Carrot, Apple, Ginger
      Juice, 113
   French Lentils with Sherry
      Vinegar, 207
   Orange and Ginger–Glazed
      Carrots, 147
   Pickled Vegetables, 172–73
   Roasted Root
      Vegetables, 145
cashews
   "Cream" of Cauliflower
      Soup, 120
   "Cream" of Mushroom
      Soup, 121
   Creamy "Cheese" Sauce, 153
   Pumpkin Pie with Pecan
      Crust, 218–19
cauliflower
   "Cream" of Cauliflower
      Soup, 120
   Pickled Vegetables, 172–73
   Roasted Broccoli au Gratin
      (substitution), 152

Roasted Cauliflower with
Tarragon and
Lemon, 169
Spicy Roasted Cauliflower
with Pimenton,
168–69
celery
Apple, Fennel, Kale
Juice, 112
Chickpeas and Spinach, 204
"Cream" of Cauliflower
Soup, 120
Cucumber, Celery, Spinach
Juice, 112
French Lentils with Sherry
Vinegar, 207
Pickled Vegetables, 172–73
celery root, *in* Roasted Root
Vegetables, 145
Chai Tea, Almond-Milk, 222
chard. *See* Swiss chard
Chayote Squash Salad with
Avocados and Arugula,
Warm, 135
"Cheese" Sauce, Creamy, 153
chewing, 37, 69–70
chickpeas. *See* garbanzo beans
children's food preferences,
101, 102–3
Chilled Couscous with
Cucumber and Mint,
198–99
Chilled Cucumber-Mint
Soup, 131
Chilled Soba Noodle Salad
with Grilled Pineapple
and Avocados, 142–43
Chocolate Coconut
Mousse, 217

chronic disease risk factors
animal-based and processed
foods, 31–33
disease prevention and
reversal, 44–46
excess sugar consumption,
38–39
inactivity, 83
poor nutrition, 75
statin drugs, 92
sugar substitutes, 40
vitamin deficiency, 47
Citrus Salad with Roasted
Fennel and
Pomegranate, 133–34
cleanse programs. *See* detox
program; Master Class
Juice Detox; Master
Cleanser (Blaine)
coconut
Chocolate Coconut
Mousse, 217
Swiss Chard with Coconut
Curry, 166
Tapioca Pudding, 215
collard greens, *in* Hearty
Greens Soup with
Farro, 122
colonics, 63–64
condiments and toppings
Egyptian Dukkah, 181
Moroccan-Spiced Apricot
Topping, 180
Pickled Vegetables, 172–73
Spiced Pumpkin Seeds, 127
Whole Roasted Garlic, 148
See also dressings and sauces
cooking
advance planning, 107–8

basic ingredients, 109
herbs and spices, 107,
243–44
methods, 241–42
reasons to cook, 100–102
salt, 111
seasonal fruits and
vegetables, 237–39
tools and equipment,
105–6, 235
unfamiliar ingredients, 106
Corn and Fire-Roasted Red
Peppers, Spring Pea
Medley with, 191
Corn Bread Stuffing,
200–201
Couscous Two Ways
Chilled Couscous with
Cucumber and Mint,
198–99
Israeli Couscous with
Sundried Tomatoes and
Kalamata Olives, 199
cranberries
French Lentils with Sherry
Vinegar, 207
Wild Rice and Bread
Stuffing, 202
cravings and food addiction,
28–30, 36–37, 70–72
"Cream" of Cauliflower
Soup, 120
"Cream" of Mushroom
Soup, 121
Creamy "Cheese" Sauce, 153
Crust, Pecan, 218
cucumbers
Apple, Fennel, Kale
Juice, 112

cucumbers *(cont.)*
  Better-Than-You've-Ever-
    Had Gazpacho,
    130–31
  Boston Bibb Salad with
    Pistachios, Meyer
    Lemon, and Cucumber
    Ribbons, 137
  Chilled Couscous with
    Cucumber and Mint,
    198–99
  Chilled Cucumber-Mint
    Soup, 131
  Cucumber, Celery, Spinach
    Juice, 112
  Pickled Vegetables,
    172–73

D

Daal, Red Lentil, 206
DeLuz, Roni, 8
desserts. *See* sweets
detox program
  attunement to body's needs,
    52–53, 72
  eating after, 67–70
  fruits during, 60
  options, 53–56
  over-the-counter cleanse
    products, 64
  preparation for, 57–59
  purpose and intention,
    56–57
  See also Master Class Juice
    Detox; Master
    Cleanser (Blaine)
Detox Soup and Broth, 117

dill, *in* Garbanzo Bean
    Lemon-Dill
    Dressing, 139
disease risk. *See* chronic
    disease risk factors
doctors and medical care
  blood tests, 47, 91–93
  consulting before juice
    cleanse, 55–56
  reliance on drugs and
    surgery, 25–27,
    35–36
  relinquishing control to,
    24–25
  selection of doctor, 88–91
dressings and sauces
  Curry Vinaigrette, 140
  Fresh Tomato Sauce, 165
  Garbanzo Bean Lemon-
    Dill Dressing, 139
  Garbanzo Bean
    Vinaigrette, 138
  Sesame-Scallion
    Dressing, 210
  Tangy BBQ Sauce, 175
drinks. *See* beverages
Dukkah, Egyptian, 181

E

eating. *See* food and
    eating
eggplant
  Eggplant Caponata, 184
  Eggplant or Asparagus
    "Takeout" with
    Chinese Garlic Sauce,
    170–71

  Mixed Veggie Grill with
    Tangy BBQ Sauce,
    174–75
  Ratatouille, 182–83
  Whole Roasted
    Eggplant, 179
Egyptian Dukkah, 181
Escarole, White Beans
    and, 205
exercise, 58, 83–85

F

farro
  Hearty Greens Soup with
    Farro, 122
  Wild Mushroom Risotto
    (substitution), 196–97
fast versus detox, 55–56
fats in processed foods, 36–37
fennel bulb
  Apple, Fennel, Kale Juice,
    112
  Citrus Salad with Roasted
    Fennel and
    Pomegranate, 133–34
fiber in plant foods, 45–46
Fire-Roasted Peppers,
    Homemade, 129
food and eating
  after cleanse, 67–69
  animal-based foods, 22,
    31–35, 73
  chewing, 37, 69–70
  children's preferences, 101,
    102–3
  cravings and addiction,
    28–30, 36–37, 70–72

emotional and social eating, 78–80, 82–83

governmental policies and guidelines, 74–76

for health, 16–19, 24, 82–83

organic and locally-produced foods, 35, 77–78

plant foods, 44–46, 69–70, 72–73

shopping guidelines, 76–78

supplements, 46–47

See also cooking; processed foods

Free-Form Vegetable Stock/Broth, 118

French Lentils with Sherry Vinegar, 207

Fresh Tomato Sauce, "Spaghetti" with Fennel Seeds and, 164–65

fruits and vegetables
cooking methods, 241–42
during detox, 60
seasonal, 237–39

Fruity Freezer Pops, 221

G

garbanzo beans
Chickpeas and Spinach, 204
Garbanzo Bean Lemon-Dill Dressing, 139
Garbanzo Bean Vinaigrette, 138
Garlic, Whole Roasted, 148

Gazpacho, Better-Than-You've-Ever-Had, 130–31

ginger
Carrot, Apple, Ginger Juice, 113
Ginger-Miso Kale, 149
Orange and Ginger–Glazed Carrots, 147

grains
Basic Brown Rice, 193
Basic Polenta, 195
Basic Quinoa, 194
Chilled Couscous with Cucumber and Mint, 198–99
Corn Bread Stuffing, 200–201
Hearty Greens Soup with Farro, 122
Israeli Couscous with Sundried Tomatoes and Kalamata Olives, 199
Seitan Bo Ssam, 209–10
Wild Mushroom Risotto, 196–97
Wild Rice and Bread Stuffing, 202

grapefruit, *in* Citrus Salad with Roasted Fennel and Pomegranate, 133–34

grapes, in Stewed Apples with Crushed Mixed Nuts, 220

green beans
Green Bean and Nicoise Olive Salad, 141

Warm Haricot Verts Salad with Butter Beans, Hazelnuts, and Curry Vinaigrette, 140

Green Leaf Juice, 113

Green Smoothie, 116

Greens Soup with Farro, Hearty, 122

Grilled Portabella Mushrooms, 161

H

Haricot Verts Salad with Butter Beans, Hazelnuts, and Curry Vinaigrette, 140

hazelnuts
Egyptian Dukkah, 181
Warm Haricot Verts Salad with Butter Beans, Hazelnuts, and Curry Vinaigrette, 140

Hearty Greens Soup with Farro, 122, 117

herbs and spices, 107, 243–44

homeostasis, 21–22, 32

hormones and antibiotics in foods, 22, 32, 33, 34

I

Iced Tea with Honey and Mint, 223

Israeli Couscous with Sundried Tomatoes and Kalamata Olives, 199

J

juice cleanse. *See* detox
    program; Master Class
    Juice Detox
juicer, to purchase, 59
juices
    Apple, Fennel, Kale Juice,
      112
    Carrot, Apple, Ginger
      Juice, 113
    Cucumber, Celery, Spinach
      Juice, 112
    Green Leaf Juice, 113
junk food. *See* processed foods

K

kale
    Apple, Fennel, Kale
      Juice, 112
    Ginger-Miso Kale, 149
    Green Smoothie, 116
    Hearty Greens Soup with
      Farro, 122
kimchi, *for* Seitan Bo Ssam,
    209–10
kitchen basics, 235. *See also*
    cooking

L

lemons
    Boston Bibb Salad with
      Pistachios, Meyer
      Lemon, and Cucumber
      Ribbons, 137

Garbanzo Bean Lemon-
    Dill Dressing, 139
Roasted Cauliflower with
    Tarragon and
    Lemon, 169
Roasted or Grilled
    Asparagus with
    Lemon, 150
lentils
    French Lentils with Sherry
      Vinegar, 207
    Red Lentil Daal, 206
locally produced foods,
    77–78

M

mangoes
    Fruity Freezer Pops, 221
    Peach Almond-Butter
      Smoothie, 115
Marinated Roasted Bell
    Peppers, 160
Marinated Wild
    Mushrooms, 185
Marrakesh-Blend Squash
    Soup, 126
Mashed Potatoes with Wild
    Mushroom Gravy,
    186–87
Master Class Juice Detox
    colonics during, 63–64
    consultation with doctor,
      55–56
    detox crisis, 62
    energy and healthy feeling,
      62–63
    versus fast, 55–56

homemade versus store-
    bought juice, 60
juice recipes, 111–13
plan, 61
rest during, 65
See also detox program
Master Cleanser (Blaine),
    5–8, 11
medical care. *See* doctors and
    medical care
Meyer Lemon, Pistachios, and
    Cucumber Ribbons,
    Boston Bibb Salad
    with, 137
mint
    Chilled Couscous with
      Cucumber and Mint,
      198–99
    Chilled Cucumber-Mint
      Soup, 131
    Iced Tea with Honey and
      Mint, 223
miso
    Ginger-Miso Kale, 149
    Sautéed Brussels Sprouts
      with White Miso and
      Sesame Seeds, 154
Mixed Veggie Grill with
    Tangy BBQ Sauce,
    174–75
Moroccan-Spiced Apricot
    Topping, 180
Mousse, Chocolate
    Coconut, 217
mushrooms
    "Cream" of Mushroom
      Soup, 121
    Grilled Portabella
      Mushrooms, 161

Marinated Wild
Mushrooms, 185
Mashed Potatoes with Wild
Mushroom Gravy,
186–87
Mixed Veggie Grill with
Tangy BBQ Sauce,
174–75
Mushroom Consommé, 123
Wild Mushroom Risotto,
196–97

N

Noodle Salad, Chilled Soba,
with Grilled Pineapple
and Avocados,
142–43
nutritional density, 8
nutritional supplements,
46–47
nuts. *See specific types*
Nuts, Crushed Mixed,
Stewed Apples
with, 220

O

olives
Green Bean and Nicoise
Olive Salad, 141
Israeli Couscous with
Sundried Tomatoes
and Kalamata
Olives, 199
Oven-Roasted Tomatoes,
163

oranges
Citrus Salad with Roasted
Fennel and
Pomegranate, 133–34
Orange and Ginger–Glazed
Carrots, 147
Red Wine–Braised
Cabbage, 156–57
organic foods, 35, 77–78
Oven-Roasted Tomatoes, 163

P

parsnips
Braised Parsnips, 146
Roasted Root
Vegetables, 145
"Pasta," Zucchini and Summer
Squash, 177
Peach Almond-Butter
Smoothie, 115
Pea Medley with Sweet Corn
and Fire-Roasted Red
Peppers, 191
pears
Stewed Apples with
Crushed Mixed
Nuts, 220
Wine-Poached Pears with
Saffron, Apricots, and
Almonds, 213–14
pecans
Corn Bread Stuffing,
200–201
Pecan Crust, 218
peppers
Homemade Fire-Roasted
Peppers, 129

Marinated Roasted Bell
Peppers, 160
Spring Pea Medley with
Sweet Corn and
Fire-Roasted Red
Peppers, 191
Tomatillo Tortilla Soup,
128–29
pesticide exposure, 77
Pesto, Walnut-Arugula,
Roasted Artichoke
Hearts with, 188–89
physical activity, 58, 83–85
Pickled Vegetables, 172–73
Pie, Pumpkin, with Pecan
Crust, 218–19
pineapple
Avocado, Pineapple, Chili,
Lime Smoothie, 116
Chilled Soba Noodle Salad
with Grilled Pineapple
and Avocados, 142–43
to cut, 116
pine nuts
Chilled Couscous with
Cucumber and Mint,
198–99
Chilled Cucumber-Mint
Soup, 131
Eggplant Caponata, 184
Marinated Roasted Bell
Peppers, 160
Pistachios, Meyer Lemon, and
Cucumber Ribbons,
Boston Bibb Salad
with, 137
plant foods
cooking methods, 241–42
health benefits, 43–46

plant foods *(cont.)*
  options, 72–73
  seasonal, 237–39
Polenta, Basic, 195
Pomegranate, Citrus Salad
  with Roasted
  Fennel and,
  133–34
Pops, Fruity Freezer, 221
Portabella Mushrooms,
  Grilled, 161
potatoes
  Green Bean and Nicoise
    Olive Salad, 141
  Mashed Potatoes with Wild
    Mushroom Gravy,
    186–87
  Purple Potato Salad with
    Whole-Grain
    Mustard, 136
  white, 144
processed foods
  chewing and swallowing, 37
  effects on health, 22–23,
    31–32
  ingredients and additives,
    35–39, 76–77, 100
Pudding, Tapioca, 215
Pumpkin Pie with Pecan
  Crust, 218–19
pumpkin seeds
  Chilled Couscous with
    Cucumber and Mint,
    198–99
  Spiced Pumpkin Seeds,
    127
  Warm Chayote Squash
    Salad with Avocados
    and Arugula, 135

Purple Potato Salad with
  Whole-Grain
  Mustard, 136

Q

Quinoa, Basic, 194

R

Ratatouille, 182–83
Red Lentil Daal, 206
Red Wine–Braised Cabbage,
  156–57
rest and relaxation
  before detox, 58
  during detox, 65
  sleep, 87–88
  stress relief, 85–86
restaurant food, 78–79, 100
rice
  Basic Brown Rice, 193
  Eggplant or Asparagus
    "Takeout" with
    Chinese Garlic Sauce,
    170–71
  Seitan Bo Ssam, 209–10
  Wild Mushroom Risotto,
    196–97
Roasted Artichoke Hearts
  with Walnut-Arugula
  Pesto, 188–89
Roasted Beets and White
  Balsamic Vinegar,
  159
Roasted Broccoli au
  Gratin, 152

Roasted Brussels Sprouts with
  Fresh Rosemary, 155
Roasted Cauliflower with
  Pimenton, Spicy,
  168–69
Roasted Cauliflower with
  Tarragon and
  Lemon, 169
Roasted Eggplant, Whole,
  179
Roasted Garlic, Whole, 148
Roasted or Grilled Asparagus
  with Lemon, 150
Root Vegetables, Roasted, 145

S

salads and dressings
  Boston Bibb Salad with
    Pistachios, Meyer
    Lemon, and Cucumber
    Ribbons, 137
  Chilled Soba Noodle Salad
    with Grilled Pineapple
    and Avocados,
    142–43
  Citrus Salad with Roasted
    Fennel and
    Pomegranate, 133–34
  Garbanzo Bean Lemon-
    Dill Dressing, 139
  Garbanzo Bean
    Vinaigrette, 138
  Green Bean and Nicoise
    Olive Salad, 141
  Purple Potato Salad with
    Whole-Grain
    Mustard, 136

Warm Chayote Squash Salad with Avocados and Arugula, 135

Warm Haricot Verts Salad with Butter Beans, Hazelnuts, and Curry Vinaigrette, 140

Salley, John, 8–9

salt, 39, 111

Sanchez, Christopher, 98

Sauce, Fresh Tomato, 165

Sauce, Tangy BBQ, 175

Sautéed Brussels Sprouts with White Miso and Sesame Seeds, 154

Scallion-Tomato Tofu Scramble, 211

Scarborough Fair Squash Soup, 125

Seitan Bo Ssam, 209–10

sesame seeds
Chilled Soba Noodle Salad with Grilled Pineapple and Avocados, 142–43
Egyptian Dukkah, 181
Sautéed Brussels Sprouts with White Miso and Sesame Seeds, 154
Sesame-Scallion Dressing, 210

Sherry Vinegar, French Lentils with, 207

shopping guidelines, 76–78

Silky Broccoli Soup, 119

smoothies
Avocado, Pineapple, Chili, Lime Smoothie, 116
Green Smoothie, 116

Peach Almond-Butter Smoothie, 115

Soba Noodle Salad with Grilled Pineapple and Avocados, Chilled, 142–43

social eating
communal cooking, 101–2
food choices, 78–80
special occasion menus, 227–28

Soulati, Sara, 9–10

soups and garnishes
Better-Than-You've-Ever-Had Gazpacho, 130–31
Butternut Squash Soup Two Ways, 124–27
Chilled Cucumber-Mint Soup, 131
"Cream" of Cauliflower Soup, 120
"Cream" of Mushroom Soup, 121
Detox Soup and Broth, 117
Free-Form Vegetable Stock/ Broth, 118
Hearty Greens Soup with Farro, 122
Homemade Fire-Roasted Peppers, 129
Marrakesh-Blend Squash Soup, 126
Mushroom Consommé, 123
Scarborough Fair Squash Soup, 125
Silky Broccoli Soup, 119
Spiced Pumpkin Seeds, 127

Tomatillo Tortilla Soup, 128–29

"Spaghetti" with Fennel Seeds and Fresh Tomato Sauce, 164–65

Spiced Pumpkin Seeds, 127

Spicy Roasted Cauliflower with Pimenton, 168–69

spinach
Chickpeas and Spinach, 204
Cucumber, Celery, Spinach Juice, 112
Green Leaf Juice, 113
Spring Pea Medley with Sweet Corn and Fire-Roasted Red Peppers, 191

squash, summer. See summer squash

squash, winter. See winter squash

Stewed Apples with Crushed Mixed Nuts, 220

strawberries, in Fruity Freezer Pops, 221

Stuffing, Corn Bread, 200–201

sugar consumption, 36, 37–39

sugar snap peas, in Spring Pea Medley with Sweet Corn and Fire-Roasted Red Peppers, 191

sugar substitutes, 40–41

summer squash
Mixed Veggie Grill with Tangy BBQ Sauce, 174–75
Ratatouille, 182–83

summer squash *(cont.)*
    Tomatillo Tortilla Soup,
      128–29
    Warm Chayote Squash
      Salad with
      Avocados and
      Arugula, 135
    Zucchini and Summer
      Squash "Pasta," 177
Sundried Tomatoes and
    Kalamata Olives,
    Israeli Couscous
    with, 199
supplements, 46–47
Sweet Potatoes with Apples,
    Candied, 190
sweets
    Almond-Milk Chai
      Tea, 222
    Chocolate Coconut
      Mousse, 217
    Fruity Freezer Pops, 221
    Pumpkin Pie with Pecan
      Crust, 218–19
    Stewed Apples with
      Crushed Mixed Nuts,
      220
    Tapioca Pudding, 215
    Wine-Poached Pears with
      Saffron, Apricots,
      and Almonds,
      213–14
Swiss chard
    Green Leaf Juice, 113
    Hearty Greens Soup with
      Farro, 122
    Swiss Chard Italiano, 167
    Swiss Chard with Coconut
      Curry, 166

T

Tangy BBQ Sauce, 175
Tapioca Pudding, 215
Tarragon and Lemon,
    Roasted Cauliflower
    with, 169
tea
    Almond-Milk Chai
      Tea, 222
    for detox, 59
    Iced Tea with Honey and
      Mint, 223
tofu
    Chocolate Coconut
      Mousse, 217
    Scallion-Tomato Tofu
      Scramble, 211
Tomatillo Tortilla Soup,
    128–29
tomatoes
    Better-Than-You've-Ever-
      Had Gazpacho,
      130–31
    to core, 130
    Fresh Tomato Sauce, 165
    Green Bean and Nicoise
      Olive Salad, 141
    Israeli Couscous with
      Sundried Tomatoes
      and Kalamata
      Olives, 199
    Oven-Roasted
      Tomatoes, 163
    Ratatouille, 182–83
    Scallion-Tomato Tofu
      Scramble, 211
    Tortilla Soup, Tomatillo,
      128–29

V

vegetables
    Free-Form Vegetable Stock/
      Broth, 118
    Mixed Veggie Grill with
      Tangy BBQ Sauce,
      174–75
    Pickled Vegetables, 172–73
    Roasted Root
      Vegetables, 145
    See also specific types
vitamin supplements, 46–47

W

walnuts
    French Lentils with Sherry
      Vinegar, 207
    Walnut-Arugula Pesto, 189
Warm Chayote Squash Salad
    with Avocados and
    Arugula, 135
Warm Haricot Verts Salad
    with Butter Beans,
    Hazelnuts, and Curry
    Vinaigrette, 140
White Beans and
    Escarole, 205
Whole Roasted Eggplant, 179
Whole Roasted Garlic, 148
wild mushrooms. *See*
    mushrooms
Wild Rice and Bread
    Stuffing, 202
Wine-Poached Pears with
    Saffron, Apricots, and
    Almonds, 213–14

winter squash
  to cut, 124
  Marrakesh-Blend Squash
    Soup, 126
  Pumpkin Pie with
    Pecan Crust,
    218–19
  Scarborough Fair Squash
    Soup, 125

"Spaghetti" with Fennel
  Seeds and Fresh
  Tomato Sauce, 164–65

Y

yellow squash. *See* summer
  squash

yucca, *in* Tomatillo
  Tortilla Soup,
  128–29

Z

zucchini. *See* summer
  squash